The Ethics of Authenticity

The Ethics of
Authenticity

Charles Taylor

Harvard University Press

Cambridge, Massachusetts

and London, England

Originally published in Canada in 1991 under the title
The Malaise of Modernity, an extended version of the
1991 Massey Lectures, which were broadcast in
November 1991 as part of CBC Radio's *Ideas* series.

This book is printed on acid-free paper.

Library of Congress Cataloging-in-Publication Data

Taylor, Charles, 1931–
The ethics of authenticity / [Charles Taylor].
p. cm.
Includes index.
ISBN 0-674-26863-6
1. Self-realization—Social aspects. 2. Civilization, Modern—
Psychological aspects. 3. Social values—History. I. Title.
BF637.S4T39 1992
320′.01—dc20

92-9179
CIP

Contents

Contents

To Bisia

Acknowledgements

My thanks go to Connie and Frank Moore for their help in discussing the project, and to Ruth Abbey and Wanda Taylor for their close reading of the manuscript. I am grateful to Eusebia da Silva for her help in defining this, and the larger project to which it belongs.

The Ethics of Authenticity

I
THREE MALAISES

I want to write here about some of the malaises of modernity. I mean by this features of our contemporary culture and society that people experience as a loss or a decline, even as our civilization "develops." Sometimes people feel that some important decline has occurred during the last years or decades — since the Second World War, or the 1950s, for instance. And sometimes the loss is felt over a much longer historical period: the whole modern era from the seventeenth century is frequently seen as the time frame of decline. Yet although the time scale can vary greatly, there is certain convergence on the themes of decline. They are often variations around a few central melodies. I want to pick out two such central themes here, and then throw in a third that largely derives from these two. These three by no means exhaust the topic, but they do get at a great deal of what troubles and perplexes us about modern society.

The worries I will be talking about are very familiar. No one needs to be reminded of them; they are discussed, bemoaned, challenged, and argued against all the time in all sorts of media. That sounds like a reason not to talk about them further. But I believe that this great familiarity hides bewilderment, that we don't really understand these changes that worry us, that the usual run of debate about them in fact misrepresents them — and thus makes us misconceive what we can do about them. The changes defining modernity are both well-known and very perplexing, and that is why it's worth talking still more about them.

(1)   The first source of worry is individualism. Of course, individualism also names what many people consider the finest achievement of modern civilization. We live in a world where people have a right to choose for themselves their own pattern of life, to decide in conscience what convictions to espouse, to determine the shape of their lives in a whole host of ways that their ancestors couldn't control. And these rights are generally defended by our legal systems. In principle, people are no longer sacrificed to the demands of supposedly sacred orders that transcend them.

Very few people want to go back on this achievement. Indeed, many think that it is still incomplete, that economic arrangements, or patterns of family life, or traditional notions of hierarchy still restrict too much our freedom to be ourselves. But many of us are also ambivalent. Modern freedom was won by our breaking loose from older moral horizons. People used to see themselves as part of a larger order. In some cases, this was a cosmic order, a "great chain of Being," in which humans figured in their proper place along with angels, heavenly bodies, and our fellow earthly creatures. This hierarchical order in the universe was reflected in the hierarchies of human society. People were often locked into a given place, a role and station that was properly theirs and from which it was almost unthinkable to deviate. Modern freedom came about through the discrediting of such orders.

But at the same time as they restricted us, these orders gave meaning to the world and to the activities of social life. The things that surround us were not just potential raw materials or instruments for our projects, but they had the significance given them by their place in the chain of being. The eagle was not just another bird, but the king of a whole domain of animal life. By the same token, the rituals and norms of society had more than merely instrumental significance. The discrediting of these orders has been called the "disenchantment" of the world. With it, things lost some of their magic.

A vigorous debate has been going on for a couple of centuries as to whether this was an unambiguously good thing. But this is not what I want to focus on here. I want to look rather at what some have seen to be the consequences for human life and meaning.

The worry has been repeatedly expressed that the individual lost something important along with the larger social and cosmic horizons of action. Some have written of this as the loss of a heroic dimension to life. People no longer have a sense of a higher purpose, of something worth dying for. Alexis de Tocqueville sometimes talked like this in the last century, referring to the "petits et vulgaires plaisirs" that people tend to seek in the democratic age.[1] In another articulation, we suffer from a lack of passion. Kierkegaard saw "the present age" in these terms. And Nietzsche's "last men" are at the final nadir of this decline; they have no aspiration left in life but to a "pitiable comfort."[2]

This loss of purpose was linked to a narrowing. People lost the broader vision because they focussed on their individual lives. Democratic equality, says Tocqueville, draws the individual towards himself, "et menace de le renfermer enfin tout entier dans la solitude de son propre coeur."[3] In other words, the dark side of individualism is a centring on the self, which both flattens and narrows our lives, makes them poorer in meaning, and less concerned with others or society.

This worry has recently surfaced again in concern at the fruits of a "permissive society," the doings of the "me generation," or the prevalence of "narcissism," to take just three of the best-known contemporary formulations. The sense that lives have been flattened and narrowed, and that this is connected to an abnormal and regrettable self-absorption, has returned in forms specific to contemporary culture. This defines the first theme I want to deal with.

(2) The disenchantment of the world is connected to another massively important phenomenon of the modern age, which also greatly troubles

many people. We might call this the primacy of instrumental reason. By "instrumental reason" I mean the kind of rationality we draw on when we calculate the most economical application of means to a given end. Maximum efficiency, the best cost-output ratio, is its measure of success.

No doubt sweeping away the old orders has immensely widened the scope of instrumental reason. Once society no longer has a sacred structure, once social arrangements and modes of action are no longer grounded in the order of things or the will of God, they are in a sense up for grabs. They can be redesigned with their consequences for the happiness and well-being of individuals as our goal. The yardstick that henceforth applies is that of instrumental reason. Similarly, once the creatures that surround us lose the significance that accrued to their place in the chain of being, they are open to being treated as raw materials or instruments for our projects.

In one way this change has been liberating. But there is also a widespread unease that instrumental reason not only has enlarged its scope but also threatens to take over our lives. The fear is that things that ought to be determined by other criteria will be decided in terms of efficiency or "cost-benefit" analysis, that the independent ends that ought to be guiding our lives will be eclipsed by the demand to maximize output. There are lots of things one can point to that give substance to this worry: for instance, the ways the demands of economic growth are used to justify very unequal distributions of wealth and income, or the way these same demands make us insensitive to the needs of the environment, even to the point of potential disaster. Or else, we can think of the way much of our social planning, in crucial areas like risk assessment, is dominated by forms of cost-benefit analysis that involve grotesque calculations, putting dollar assessments on human lives.[4]

The primacy of instrumental reason is also evident in the prestige and aura that surround technology, and makes us believe that we should seek technological solutions even when something very different is called for. We see this often enough in the realm of politics, as Bellah and his colleagues forcefully argue in their new book.[5] But it also invades other domains, such as medicine. Patricia Benner has argued in a number of important works that the technological approach in medicine has often sidelined the kind of care that involves treating the patient as a whole person with a life story, and not as the locus of a technical problem. Society and the medical establishment frequently undervalue the contribution of nurses, who more often than not provide this humanly sensitive caring, as against that of specialists with high-tech knowledge.[6]

The dominant place of technology is also thought to have contributed to the narrowing and flattening of our lives that I have just been discussing in connection with the first theme. People have spoken of a loss of resonance, depth, or richness in our human surroundings. Almost 150 years ago, Marx, in the *Communist Manifesto*, remarked that one of the results of capitalist development was that "all that is solid melts in air." The claim is that the solid, lasting, often expressive objects that served us in the past are being set aside for the quick, shoddy, replaceable

commodities with which we now surround ourselves. Albert Borgman speaks of the "device paradigm," whereby we withdraw more and more from
"manifold engagement" with our environment and
instead request and get products designed to deliver
some circumscribed benefit. He contrasts what is
involved in heating our homes, with the contemporary central heating furnace, with what this same
function entailed in pioneer times, when the whole
family had to be involved in cutting and stacking the
wood and feeding the stove or fireplace.[7] Hannah
Arendt focussed on the more and more ephemeral
quality of modern objects of use and argued that
"the reality and reliability of the human world rest
primarily on the fact that we are surrounded by
things more permanent than the activity by which
they are produced."[8] This permanence comes under
threat in a world of modern commodities.

This sense of threat is increased by the knowledge
that this primacy is not just a matter of a perhaps
unconscious orientation, which we are prodded and
tempted into by the modern age. As such it would
be hard enough to combat, but at least it might yield
to persuasion. But it is also clear that powerful
mechanisms of social life press us in this direction.
A manager in spite of her own orientation may be
forced by the conditions of the market to adopt a
maximizing strategy she feels is destructive. A bu-
reaucrat, in spite of his personal insight, may be
forced by the rules under which he operates to make
a decision he knows to be against humanity and
good sense.

Marx and Weber and other great theorists have

explored these impersonal mechanisms, which
Weber has designated by the evocative term of "the
iron cage." And some people have wanted to draw
from these analyses the conclusion that we are utterly helpless in the face of such forces, or at least
helpless unless we totally dismantle the institutional
structures under which we have been operating for
the last centuries — that is, the market and the state.
This aspiration seems so unrealizable today that it
amounts to declaring us helpless.

I want to return to this below, but I believe that
these strong theories of fatality are abstract and
wrong. Our degrees of freedom are not zero. There
is a point to deliberating what ought to be our ends,
and whether instrumental reason ought to have a
lesser role in our lives than it does. But the truth in
these analyses is that it is not just a matter of changing the outlook of individuals, it is not just a battle
of "hearts and minds," important as this is. Change
in this domain will have to be institutional as well,
even though it cannot be as sweeping and total as
the great theorists of revolution proposed.

(3) This brings us to the political level, and to the
feared consequences for political life of individualism and instrumental reason. One I have already
introduced. It is that the institutions and structures
of industrial-technological society severely restrict
our choices, that they force societies as well as individuals to give a weight to instrumental reason that
in serious moral deliberation we would never do,
and which may even be highly destructive. A case
in point is our great difficulties in tackling even vital
threats to our lives from environmental disasters,

like the thinning ozone layer. The society structured around instrumental reason can be seen as imposing a great loss of freedom, on both individuals and the group — because it is not just our social decisions that are shaped by these forces. An individual lifestyle is also hard to sustain against the grain. For instance, the whole design of some modern cities makes it hard to function without a car, particularly where public transport has been eroded in favour of the private automobile.

But there is another kind of loss of freedom, which has also been widely discussed, most memorably by Alexis de Tocqueville. A society in which people end up as the kind of individuals who are "enclosed in their own hearts" is one where few will want to participate actively in self-government. They will prefer to stay at home and enjoy the satisfactions of private life, as long as the government of the day produces the means to these satisfactions and distributes them widely.

This opens the danger of a new, specifically modern form of despotism, which Tocqueville calls "soft" despotism. It will not be a tyranny of terror and oppression as in the old days. The government will be mild and paternalistic. It may even keep democratic forms, with periodic elections. But in fact, everything will be run by an "immense tutelary power,"⁹ over which people will have little control. The only defence against this, Tocqueville thinks, is a vigorous political culture in which participation is valued, at several levels of government and in voluntary associations as well. But the atomism of the self-absorbed individual militates against this. Once participation declines, once the lateral associations that were its vehicles wither away, the individual citizen is left alone in the face of the vast bureaucratic state and feels, correctly, powerless. This demotivates the citizen even further, and the vicious cycle of soft despotism is joined.

Perhaps something like this alienation from the public sphere and consequent loss of political control is happening in our highly centralized and bureaucratic political world. Many contemporary thinkers have seen Tocqueville's work as prophetic.[10] If this is so, what we are in danger of losing is political control over our destiny, something we could exercise in common as citizens. This is what Tocqueville called "political liberty." What is threatened here is our dignity as citizens. The impersonal mechanisms mentioned above may reduce our degrees of freedom as a society, but the loss of political liberty would mean that even the choices left would no longer be made by ourselves as citizens, but by irresponsible tutelary power.

These, then, are the three malaises about modernity that I want to deal with in this book. The first fear is about what we might call a loss of meaning, the fading of moral horizons. The second concerns the eclipse of ends, in face of rampant instrumental reason. And the third is about a loss of freedom.

Of course, these are not uncontroversial. I have spoken about worries that are widespread and mentioned influential authors, but nothing here is agreed. Even those who share some form of these worries dispute vigorously how they should be formulated. And there are lots of people who want to dismiss them out of hand. Those who are deeply into what the critics call the "culture of narcissism" think of the objectors as hankering for an earlier, more oppressive age. Adepts of modern technological reason think the critics of the primacy of the instrumental are reactionary and obscurantist, scheming to deny the world the benefits of science. And there are proponents of mere negative freedom who believe that the value of political liberty is overblown, and that a society in which scientific management combines with maximum independence for each individual is what we ought to aim at. Modernity has its boosters as well as its knockers.

Nothing is agreed here, and the debate continues. But in the course of this debate, the essential nature of the developments, which are here being decried, there being praised, is often misunderstood. And as a result, the real nature of the moral choices to be made is obscured. In particular, I will claim that the right path to take is neither that recommended by straight boosters nor that favoured by outright knockers. Nor will a simple trade-off between the advantages and costs of, say, individualism, technology, and bureaucratic management provide the answer. The nature of modern culture is more subtle and complex than this. I want to claim that both boosters and knockers are right, but in a way that can't be done justice to by a simple trade-off between advantages and costs. There is in fact both much that is admirable and much that is debased and frightening in all the developments I have been describing, but to understand the relation between the two is to see that the issue is not how much of a price in bad consequences you have to pay for the positive fruits, but rather how to steer these developments towards their greatest promise and avoid the slide into the debased forms.

Now I have nothing like the space I would need to treat all three of these themes as they deserve, so I propose a short-cut. I will launch into a discussion of the first theme, concerning the dangers of individualism and the loss of meaning. I will pursue this discussion at some length. Having derived some idea of how this issue ought to be treated, I will suggest how a similar treatment of the other two might run. The bulk of the discussion will therefore concentrate on the first axis of concern. Let us examine in more detail what form this arises in today.

II
THE INARTICULATE DEBATE

We can pick it up through a very influential recent book in the United States, Allan Bloom's *The Closing of the American Mind*. The book itself was a rather remarkable phenomenon: a work by an academic political theorist about the climate of opinion among today's students, it held a place on the *New York Times* best-seller list for several months, greatly to the surprise of the author. It touched a chord.

The stance it took was severely critical of today's educated youth. The main feature it noted in their outlook on life was their acceptance of a rather facile relativism. Everybody has his or her own "values," and about these it is impossible to argue. But as Bloom noted, this was not just an epistemological position, a view about the limits of what reason can establish; it was also held as a moral position: one ought not to challenge another's values. That is their concern, their life choice, and it ought to be respected. The relativism was partly grounded in a principle of mutual respect.

In other words, the relativism was itself an offshoot of a form of individualism, whose principle is something like this: everyone has a right to develop their own form of life, grounded on their own sense of what is really important or of value. People are called upon to be true to themselves and to seek their own self-fulfilment. What this consists of, each must, in the last instance, determine for him- or herself. No one else can or should try to dictate its content.

This is a familiar enough position today. It reflects what we could call the individualism of self-fulfilment, which is widespread in our times and has grown particularly strong in Western societies since the 1960s. It has been picked up on and discussed in other influential books: Daniel Bell's *The Cultural Contradictions of Capitalism*, Christopher Lasch's *The Culture of Narcissism* and *The Minimal Self*, and Gilles Lipovetsky's *L'ère du vide*.

The tone of concern is audible in all these, although perhaps less marked in Lipovetsky. It runs roughly along the lines I outlined above under theme 1. This individualism involves a centring on the self and a concomitant shutting out, or even unawareness, of the greater issues or concerns that transcend the self, be they religious, political, historical. As a consequence, life is narrowed or flattened.[11] And the worry characteristically spills over into the third area I described: these authors are concerned about the possibly dire political consequences of this shift in the culture.

Now there is much that I agree with in the strictures these writers make of contemporary culture. As I shall explain in a minute, I think the relativism widely espoused today is a profound mistake, even in some respects self-stultifying. It seems true that the culture of self-fulfilment has led many people to lose sight of concerns that transcend them. And it seems obvious that it has taken trivialized and self-indulgent forms. This can even result in a sort of absurdity, as new modes of conformity arise among people who are striving to be themselves, and beyond this, new forms of dependence, as people insecure in their identities turn to all sorts of self-appointed experts and guides, shrouded with the prestige of science or some exotic spirituality.

But there is something I nevertheless want to resist in the thrust of the arguments that these authors present. It emerges clearest in Bloom, perhaps most strongly in his tone of contempt for the culture he is describing. He doesn't seem to recognize that there is a powerful moral ideal at work here, however debased and travestied its expression might be. The moral ideal behind self-fulfilment is that of being true to oneself, in a specifically modern understanding of that term. A couple of decades ago, this was brilliantly defined by Lionel Trilling in an influential book, in which he encapsulated that modern form and distinguished it from earlier ones. The distinction is expressed in the title of the book, *Sincerity and*

Authenticity, and following him I am going to use the
term "authenticity" for the contemporary ideal.

What do I mean by a moral ideal? I mean a picture
of what a better or higher mode of life would be,
where "better" and "higher" are defined not in
terms of what we happen to desire or need, but offer
a standard of what we ought to desire.

The force of terms like "narcissism" (Lasch's
word), or "hedonism" (Bell's description), is to
imply that there is no moral ideal at work here; or if
there is, on the surface, that it should rather be seen
as a screen for self-indulgence. As Bloom puts it,
"The great majority of students, although they as
much as anyone want to think well of themselves,
are aware that they are busy with their own careers
and their relationships. There is a certain rhetoric of
self-fulfilment that gives a patina of glamor to this
life, but they can see that there is nothing particularly noble about it. Survivalism has taken the place
of heroism as the admired quality."[12] I have no doubt
that this describes some, perhaps lots, of people, but
it is a big mistake to think that it allows us insight
into the change in our culture, into the power of this
moral ideal — which we need to understand if we
are to explain even why it is used as a hypocritical
"patina" by the self-indulgent.

What we need to understand here is the moral
force behind notions like self-fulfilment. Once we
try to explain this simply as a kind of egoism, or a
species of moral laxism, a self-indulgence with regard to a tougher, more exigent earlier age, we are
already off the track. Talk of "permissiveness"
misses this point. Moral laxity there is, and our age

is not alone in this. What we need to explain is what is peculiar to our time. It's not just that people sacrifice their love relationships, and the care of their children, to pursue their careers. Something like this has perhaps always existed. The point is that today many people feel *called* to do this, feel they ought to do this, feel their lives would be somehow wasted or unfulfilled if they didn't do it.

Thus what gets lost in this critique is the moral force of the ideal of authenticity. It is somehow being implicitly discredited, along with its contemporary forms. That would not be so bad if we could turn to the opposition for a defence. But here we will be disappointed. That the espousal of authenticity takes the form of a kind of soft relativism means that the vigorous defence of any moral ideal is somehow off limits. For the implications, as I have just described them above, are that some forms of life are indeed *higher* than others, and the culture of tolerance for individual self-fulfilment shies away from these claims. This means, as has often been pointed out, that there is something contradictory and self-defeating in their position, since the relativism itself is powered (at least partly) by a moral ideal. But consistently or not, this is the position usually adopted. The ideal sinks to the level of an axiom, something one doesn't challenge but also never expounds.

In adopting the ideal, people in the culture of authenticity, as I want to call it, give support to a certain kind of liberalism, which has been espoused by many others as well. This is the liberalism of neutrality. One of its basic tenets is that a liberal society must be neutral on questions of what constitutes a good life. The good life is what each individual seeks, in his or her own way, and government would be lacking in impartiality, and thus in equal respect for all citizens, if it took sides on this question.[13] Although many of the writers in this school are passionate opponents of soft relativism (Dworkin and Kymlicka among them), the result of their theory is to banish discussions about the good life to the margins of political debate.

The result is an extraordinary inarticulacy about one of the constitutive ideals of modern culture.[14] Its opponents slight it, and its friends can't speak of it. The whole debate conspires to put it in the shade, to render it invisible. This has detrimental consequences. But before going on to these, I want to mention two other factors that conspire to intensify this silence.

One of them is the hold of moral subjectivism in our culture. By this I mean the view that moral positions are not in any way grounded in reason or the nature of things but are ultimately just adopted by each of us because we find ourselves drawn to them. On this view, reason can't adjudicate moral disputes. Of course, you can point out to someone certain consequences of his position he may not have thought about. So the critics of authenticity can point to the possible social and political results of each person seeking self-fulfilment. But if your interlocutor still feels like holding to his original position, nothing further can be said to gainsay him.

The grounds for this view are complex and go far beyond the moral reasons for soft relativism, although subjectivism clearly provides an important backing for this relativism. Obviously, lots of people into the contemporary culture of authenticity are happy to espouse this understanding of the role (or non-role) of reason. What is perhaps more surprising, so are a great many of their opponents, who therefore are led to despair all the more of reforming contemporary culture. If the youth really don't care for causes that transcend the self, then what can you say to them?

Of course, there are critics who hold that there are standards in reason.[15] They think that there is such a thing as human nature, and that an understanding of this will show certain ways of life to be right and others wrong, certain ways to be higher and better than others. The philosophical roots of this position are in Aristotle. By contrast, modern subjectivists tend to be very critical of Aristotle, and complain that his "metaphysical biology" is out of date and thoroughly unbelievable today.

But philosophers who think like this have generally been opponents of the ideal of authenticity; they have seen it as part of a mistaken departure from the standards rooted in human nature. They had no reason to articulate what it is about; while those who upheld it have been frequently discouraged from doing so by their subjectivist views.

A third factor that has obscured the importance of authenticity as a moral ideal has been the normal fashion of social science explanation. This has generally shied away from invoking moral ideals and has tended to have recourse to supposedly harder and more down to earth factors in its explanation. And so the features of modernity I have been focussing on here, individualism and the expansion of instrumental reason, have often been accounted for as by-products of social change: for instance, as spin-offs from industrialization, or greater mobility, or urbanization. There are certainly important causal relations to be traced here, but the accounts that invoke them frequently skirt altogether the issue whether these changes in culture and outlook owe anything to their own inherent power as moral ideals. The implicit answer is often negative.[16]

Of course, the social changes that are supposed to spawn the new outlook must themselves be explained, and this will involve some recourse to human motivations, unless we suppose that industrialization or the growth of cities occurred entirely in a fit of absence of mind. We need some notion of what moved people to push steadily in one direction, for example towards the greater application of technology to production, or towards greater concentrations of population. But what are often invoked are motivations that are non-moral. By that I mean motivations that can actuate people quite without connection to any moral ideal, as I defined this earlier. So we very often find these social changes explained in terms of the desire for greater wealth, or power, or the means of survival or control over others. Though all these things can be woven into moral ideals, they need not be, and so explanation in terms of them is considered sufficiently "hard" and "scientific."

Even where individual freedom and the enlargement of instrumental reason are seen as ideas whose intrinsic attractions can help explain their rise, this attraction is frequently understood in non-moral terms. That is, the power of these ideas is often understood not in terms of their moral force but just because of the advantages they seem to bestow on people regardless of their moral outlook, or even whether they have a moral outlook. Freedom allows you to do what you want, and the greater application of instrumental reason gets you more of what you want, whatever that is.[17]

The result of all this has been to thicken the darkness around the moral ideal of authenticity. Critics of contemporary culture tend to disparage it as an ideal, even to confound it with a non-moral desire to do what one wants without interference. The defenders of this culture are pushed into inarticulacy about it by their own outlook. The general force of subjectivism in our philosophical world and the power of neutral liberalism intensify the sense that these issues can't and shouldn't be talked about. And then on top of it all, social science seems to be telling us that to understand such phenomena as the contemporary culture of authenticity, we shouldn't have recourse in our explanations to such things as moral ideals but should see it all in terms of, say, recent changes in the mode of production,[18] or new patterns of youth consumption, or the security of affluence.

Does this matter? I think so, very much. Many of the things critics of contemporary culture attack are debased and deviant forms of this ideal. That is, they flow from it, and their practitioners invoke it, but in fact they don't represent an authentic (!) fulfilment of it. Soft relativism is a case in point. Bloom sees that it has a moral basis: "The relativity of truth is not a theoretical insight but a moral postulate, the condition of a free society, or so [the students] see it."[19] But in fact, I would like to claim, it travesties and eventually betrays this moral insight. So far from being a reason to reject the moral ideal of authenticity, it should itself be rejected in its name. Or so I would like to argue.

A similar point can be made for those appeals to authenticity that justify ignoring whatever transcends the self: for rejecting our past as irrelevant, or denying the demands of citizenship, or the duties of solidarity, or the needs of the natural environment. Similarly, justifying in the name of authenticity a concept of relationships as instrumental to individual self-fulfilment should also be seen as a self-stultifying travesty. The affirmation of the power of choice as itself a good to be maximized is a deviant product of the ideal.

Now if something like this is true, then it matters to be able to say it. For then one *has* something to say, in all reason, to the people who invest their lives in these deviant forms. And this may make a difference to their lives. Some of these things may be heard. Articulacy here has a moral point, not just in correcting what may be wrong views but also in making the force of an ideal that people are already living by more palpable, more vivid for them; and by making it more vivid, empowering them to live up to it in a fuller and more integral fashion.

What I am suggesting is a position distinct from both boosters and knockers of contemporary culture. Unlike the boosters, I do not believe that everything is as it should be in this culture. Here I tend to agree with the knockers. But unlike them, I think that authenticity should be taken seriously as a moral ideal. I differ also from the various middle positions, which hold that there are some good things in this culture (like greater freedom for the individual), but that these come at the expense of certain dangers (like a weakening of the sense of citizenship), so that one's best policy is to find the ideal point of trade-off between advantages and costs.

The picture I am offering is rather that of an ideal that has degraded but that is very worthwhile in itself, and indeed, I would like to say, unrepudiable by moderns. So what we need is neither root-and-branch condemnation nor uncritical praise; and not a carefully balanced trade-off. What we need is a work of retrieval, through which this ideal can help us restore our practice.

To go along with this, you have to believe three things, all controversial: (1) that authenticity is a valid ideal; (2) that you can argue in reason about ideals and about the conformity of practices to these ideals; and (3) that these arguments can make a difference. The first belief flies in the face of the major thrust of criticism of the culture of authenticity, the second involves rejecting subjectivism, and the third is incompatible with those accounts of modernity that see us as imprisoned in modern culture by the "system," whether this is defined as capitalism, industrial society, or bureaucracy. I hope to be able to make some of this plausible in what follows. Let me start with the ideal.

III
THE SOURCES OF
AUTHENTICITY

The ethic of authenticity is something relatively new and peculiar to modern culture. Born at the end of the eighteenth century, it builds on earlier forms of individualism, such as the individualism of disengaged rationality, pioneered by Descartes, where the demand is that each person think self-responsibly for him- or herself, or the political individualism of Locke, which sought to make the person and his or her will prior to social obligation. But authenticity also has been in some respects in conflict with these earlier forms. It is a child of the Romantic period, which was critical of disengaged rationality and of an atomism that didn't recognize the ties of community.

One way of describing its development is to see its starting point in the eighteenth-century notion that human beings are endowed with a moral sense, an intuitive feeling for what is right and wrong. The original point of this doctrine was to combat a rival view, that knowing right and wrong was a matter of calculating consequences, in particular those concerned with divine reward and punishment. The notion was that understanding right and wrong was not a matter of dry calculation, but was anchored in our feelings. Morality has, in a sense, a voice within.[20]

The notion of authenticity develops out of a displacement of the moral accent in this idea. On the original view, the inner voice is important because it tells us what is the right thing to do. Being in touch with our moral feelings would matter here, as a means to the end of acting rightly. What I'm calling the displacement of the moral accent comes about when being in touch takes on independent and crucial moral significance. It comes to be something we have to attain to be true and full human beings.

To see what is new in this, we have to see the analogy to earlier moral views, where being in touch with some source — God, say, or the Idea of the Good — was considered essential to full being. Only now the source we have to connect with is deep in us. This is part of the massive subjective turn of modern culture, a new form of inwardness, in which we come to think of ourselves as beings with inner depths. At first, this idea that the source is within doesn't exclude our being related to God or the Ideas; it can be considered our proper way to them. In a sense, it can be seen just as a continuation and intensification of the development inaugurated by Saint Augustine, who saw the road to God as passing through our own reflexive awareness of ourselves.

The first variants of this new view were theistic, or at least pantheist. This is illustrated by the most important philosophical writer who helped to bring about this change, Jean Jacques Rousseau. I think Rousseau is important not because he inaugurated the change; rather I would argue that his great popularity comes in part from his articulating something that was already happening in the culture. Rousseau frequently presents the issue of morality as that of our following a voice of nature within us. This voice is most often drowned out by the passions induced by our dependence on others, of which the key one is "amour propre" or pride. Our moral salvation comes from recovering authentic moral contact with ourselves. Rousseau even gives a name to the intimate contact with oneself, more fundamental than any moral view, that is a source of joy and contentment: "le sentiment de l'existence."[21]

Rousseau also articulated a closely related idea in a most influential way. This is the notion of what I want to call self-determining freedom. It is the idea that I am free when I decide for myself what concerns me, rather than being shaped by external influences. It is a standard of freedom that obviously goes beyond what has been called negative liberty, where I am free to do what I want without interference by others because that is compatible with my being shaped and influenced by society and its laws of conformity. Self-determining freedom demands that I break the hold of all such external impositions, and decide for myself alone.

I mention this here not because it is essential to authenticity. Obviously the two ideals are distinct. But they have developed together, sometimes in the works of the same authors, and their relations have been complex, sometimes at odds, sometimes closely bound together. As a result, they have often been confused, and this has been one of the sources of the deviant forms of authenticity, as I shall argue. I will return to this later.

Self-determining freedom has been an idea of immense power in our political life. In Rousseau's work it takes political form, in the notion of a social contract state founded on a general will, which precisely because it is the form of our common freedom can brook no opposition in the name of freedom. This idea has been one of the intellectual sources of modern totalitarianism, starting, one might argue, with the Jacobins. And although Kant reinterpreted this notion of freedom in purely moral terms, as autonomy, it returns to the political sphere with a vengeance with Hegel and Marx.

But to return to the ideal of authenticity: it becomes crucially important because of a development that occurs after Rousseau and that I associate with Herder — once again its major early articulator rather than its originator. Herder put forward the idea that each of us has an original way of being human. Each person has his or her own "measure" is his way of putting it.[22] This idea has entered very deep into modern consciousness. It is also new. Before the late eighteenth century no one thought that the differences between human beings had this kind of moral significance. There is a certain way of being human that is *my* way. I am called upon to live my life in this way, and not in imitation of anyone else's. But this gives a new importance to being true to myself. If I am not, I miss the point of my life, I miss what being human is for *me*.

This is the powerful moral ideal that has come down to us. It accords crucial moral importance to a kind of contact with myself, with my own inner nature, which it sees as in danger of being lost, partly through the pressures towards outward conformity, but also because in taking an instrumental stance to myself, I may have lost the capacity to listen to this inner voice. And then it greatly increases the importance of this self-contact by introducing the principle of originality: each of our voices has something of its own to say. Not only should I not fit my life to the demands of external conformity; I can't even find the model to live by outside myself. I can find it only within.

Being true to myself means being true to my own originality, and that is something only I can articulate and discover. In articulating it, I am also defining myself. I am realizing a potentiality that is properly my own. This is the background understanding to the modern ideal of authenticity, and to the goals of self-fulfilment or self-realization in which it is usually couched. This is the background that gives moral force to the culture of authenticity, including its most degraded, absurd, or trivialized forms. It is what gives sense to the idea of "doing your own thing" or "finding your own fulfilment."

IV
INESCAPABLE HORIZONS

*T*his is a very rapid sketch of the origins of authenticity. I shall have to fill in more detail later. But for the moment it is enough to see what is involved in reasoning here. And so I want to take up the second controversial claim that I made at the end of the last section. Can one say anything in reason to people who are immersed in the contemporary culture of authenticity? Can you talk in reason to people who are deeply into soft relativism, or who seem to accept no allegiance higher than their own development — say, those who seem ready to throw away love, children, democratic solidarity, for the sake of some career advancement?

Well, how do we reason? Reasoning in moral matters is always reasoning with somebody. You have an interlocutor, and you start from where that person is, or with the actual difference between you; you don't reason from the ground up, as though you were talking to someone who recognized no moral demands whatever. A person who accepted no moral demands would be as impossible to argue with about right and wrong as would a person who refused to accept the world of perception around us be impossible to argue with about empirical matters.[23]

But we are imagining discussing with people who are in the contemporary culture of authenticity. And that means that they are trying to shape their lives in the light of this ideal. We are not left with just the bare facts of their preferences. But if we start from the ideal, then we can ask: What are the conditions in human life of realizing an ideal of this kind? And what does the ideal properly understood call for? The two orders of questions interweave, or perhaps shade into each other. In the second, we are trying to define better what the ideal consists in. With the first, we want to bring out certain general features of human life that condition the fulfilment of this or any other ideal.

In what follows, I want to work out two lines of argument that can illustrate what is involved in this kind of questioning. The argument will be very sketchy, more in the nature of a suggestion of what a convincing demonstration might look like. The aim will be to give some plausibility to my second claim, that you can argue in reason about these matters, and hence to show that there is indeed a practical point in trying to understand better what authenticity consists in.

The general feature of human life that I want to

evoke is its fundamentally *dialogical* character. We become full human agents, capable of understanding ourselves, and hence of defining an identity, through our acquisition of rich human languages of expression. For purposes of this discussion, I want to take "language" in a broad sense, covering not only the words we speak but also other modes of expression whereby we define ourselves, including the "languages" of art, of gesture, of love, and the like. But we are inducted into these in exchange with others. No one acquires the languages needed for self-definition on their own. We are introduced to them through exchanges with others who matter to us — what George Herbert Mead called "significant others."[24] The genesis of the human mind is in this sense not "monological," not something each accomplishes on his or her own, but dialogical.

Moreover, this is not just a fact about *genesis*, which can be ignored later on. It's not just that we learn the languages in dialogue and then can go on to use them for our own purposes on our own. This describes our situation to some extent in our culture. We are expected to develop our own opinions, outlook, stances to things, to a considerable degree through solitary reflection. But this is not how things work with important issues, such as the definition of our identity. We define this always in dialogue with, sometimes in struggle against, the identities our significant others want to recognize in us. And even when we outgrow some of the latter — our parents, for instance — and they disappear from our lives, the conversation with them continues within us as long as we live.[25]

So the contribution of significant others, even when it occurs at the beginning of our lives, continues throughout. Some people might be following me up to here, but still want to hold on to some form of the monological ideal. True, we can never liberate ourselves completely from those whose love and care shaped us early in life, but we should strive to define ourselves on our own to the fullest degree possible, coming as best we can to understand and thus gain some control over the influence of our parents, and avoiding falling into any further such dependencies. We will need relationships to fulfil but not to define ourselves.

This is a common ideal, but I think it seriously underestimates the place of the dialogical in human life. It still wants to confine it as much as possible to the genesis. It forgets how our understanding of the good things in life can be transformed by our enjoying them in common with people we love, how some goods become accessible to us only through such common enjoyment. Because of this, it would take a great deal of effort, and probably many wrenching break-ups, to *prevent* our identity being formed by the people we love. Consider what we mean by "identity." It is "who" we are, "where we're coming from." As such it is the background against which our tastes and desires and opinions and aspirations make sense. If some of the things I value most are accessible to me only in relation to the person I love, then she becomes internal to my identity.

To some people this might seem a limitation, from which one might aspire to free oneself. This is one way of understanding the impulse behind the life of the hermit, or to take a case more familiar to our culture, the solitary artist. But from another perspective, we might see even this as aspiring to a certain kind of dialogicality. In the case of the hermit, the interlocutor is God. In the case of the solitary artist, the work itself is addressed to a future audience, perhaps still to be created by the work itself. The very form of a work of art shows its character as *addressed*.[26] But however one feels about it, the making and sustaining of our identity, in the absence of a heroic effort to break out of ordinary existence, remains dialogical throughout our lives.

I want to indicate below that this central fact has been recognized in the growing culture of authenticity. But what I want to do now is take this dialogical feature of our condition, on one hand, and certain demands inherent in the ideal of authenticity on the other, and show that the more self-centred and "narcissistic" modes of contemporary culture are manifestly inadequate. More particularly, I want to show that modes that opt for self-fulfilment without regard (a) to the demands of our ties with others or (b) to demands of any kind emanating from something more or other than human desires or aspirations are self-defeating, that they destroy the conditions for realizing authenticity itself. I'll take these in reverse order, and start with (b), arguing from the demands of authenticity itself as an ideal.

(1) When we come to understand what it is to define ourselves, to determine in what our originality consists, we see that we have to take as background some sense of what is significant. Defining myself means finding what is significant in my dif-

ference from others. I may be the only person with
exactly 3,732 hairs on my head, or be exactly the
same height as some tree on the Siberian plain, but
so what? If I begin to say that I define myself by my
ability to articulate important truths, or play the
Hammerklavier like no one else, or revive the tradition of my ancestors, then we are in the domain of
recognizable self-definitions.

The difference is plain. We understand right away
that the latter properties have human significance, or
can easily be seen by people to have this, whereas the
former do not — not, that is, without some special
story. Perhaps the number 3,732 is a sacred one in some
society; then having this number of hairs can be significant. But we get to this by linking it to the sacred.

We saw above in the second section how the
contemporary culture of authenticity slides towards
soft relativism. This gives further force to a general
presumption of subjectivism about value: things
have significance not of themselves but because people deem them to have it — as though people could
determine what is significant, either by decision, or
perhaps unwittingly and unwillingly by just feeling
that way. This is crazy. I couldn't just *decide* that the
most significant action is wiggling my toes in warm
mud. Without a special explanation, this is not an
intelligible claim (like the 3,732 hairs above). So I
wouldn't know what sense to attribute to someone
allegedly *feeling* that this was so. What could someone *mean* who said this?

But if it makes sense only with an explanation
(perhaps mud is the element of the world spirit,
which you contact with your toes), it is open to

criticism. What if the explanation is wrong, doesn't pan out, or can be replaced with a better account? Your feeling a certain way can never be sufficient grounds for respecting your position, because your feeling can't *determine* what is significant. Soft relativism self-destructs.

Things take on importance against a background of intelligibility. Let us call this a horizon. It follows that one of the things we can't do, if we are to define ourselves significantly, is suppress or deny the horizons against which things take on significance for us. This is the kind of self-defeating move frequently being carried out in our subjectivist civilization. In stressing the legitimacy of choice between certain options, we very often find ourselves depriving the options of their significance. For instance, there is a certain discourse of justification of non-standard sexual orientations. People want to argue that heterosexual monogamy is not the only way to achieve sexual fulfilment, that those who are inclined to homosexual relations, for instance, shouldn't feel themselves embarked on a lesser, less worthy path. This fits well into the modern understanding of authenticity, with its notion of difference, originality, of the acceptance of diversity. I will try to say more about these connections below. But however we explain it, it is clear that a rhetoric of "difference," of "diversity" (even "multiculturalism"), is central to the contemporary culture of authenticity.

But in some forms this discourse slides towards an affirmation of choice itself. All options are equally worthy, because they are freely chosen, and it is choice that confers worth. The subjectivist principle

underlying soft relativism is at work here. But this
implicitly denies the existence of a pre-existing horizon of significance, whereby some things are
worthwhile and others less so, and still others not at
all, quite anterior to choice. But then the choice of
sexual orientation loses any special significance. It
is on a level with any other preferences, like that for
taller or shorter sexual partners, or blonds or bru-
nettes. No one would dream of making discriminat-
ing judgements about these preferences, but that's
because they are all without importance. They really
do just depend on how you feel. Once sexual orientation comes to be assimilated to these, which is what
happens when one makes *choice* the crucial justifying
reason, the original goal, which was to assert the
equal value of this orientation, is subtly frustrated.
Difference so asserted becomes *insignificant*.

Asserting the value of a homosexual orientation
has to be done differently, more empirically, one
might say, taking into account the actual nature of
homo- and heterosexual experience and life. It can't
just be assumed a priori, on the grounds that anything we choose is all right.

In this case, the assertion of value is contaminated
by its connection with another leading idea, which
I have mentioned above as closely interwoven with
authenticity, that of self-determining freedom. This
is partly responsible for the accent on choice as a
crucial consideration, and also for the slide towards
soft relativism. I will return to this below, in talking
about how the goal of authenticity comes to deviate.

But for the moment, the general lesson is that
authenticity can't be defended in ways that collapse

horizons of significance. Even the sense that the significance of my life comes from its being chosen — the case where authenticity is actually grounded on self-determining freedom — depends on the understanding that *independent of my will* there is something noble, courageous, and hence significant in giving shape to my own life. There is a picture here of what human beings are like, placed between this option for self-creation, and easier modes of copping out, going with the flow, conforming with the masses, and so on, which picture is seen as true, discovered, not decided. Horizons are given.

But more: this minimum degree of givenness, which underpins the importance of choice, is not sufficient as a horizon, as we saw with the example of sexual orientation. It may be important that my life be chosen, as John Stuart Mill asserts in *On Liberty*,[27] but unless some options are more significant than others, the very idea of self-choice falls into triviality and hence incoherence. Self-choice as an ideal makes sense only because some *issues* are more significant than others. I couldn't claim to be a self-chooser, and deploy a whole Nietzschean vocabulary of self-making, just because I choose steak and fries over poutine for lunch. Which issues are significant, *I* do not determine. If I did, no issue would be significant. But then the very ideal of self-choosing *as a moral ideal* would be impossible.

So the ideal of self-choice supposes that there are *other* issues of significance beyond self-choice. The ideal couldn't stand alone, because it requires a horizon of issues of importance, which help define the *respects* in which self-making is significant. Following Nietzsche, I am indeed a truly great philosopher if I remake the table of values. But this means redefining values concerning important questions, not redesigning the menu at McDonald's, or next year's casual fashion.

The agent seeking significance in life, trying to define him- or herself meaningfully, has to exist in a horizon of important questions. That is what is self-defeating in modes of contemporary culture that concentrate on self-fulfilment *in opposition* to the demands of society, or nature, which *shut out* history and the bonds of solidarity. These self-centred "narcissistic" forms are indeed shallow and trivialized; they are "flattened and narrowed," as Bloom says. But this is not because they belong to the culture of authenticity. Rather it is because they fly in the face of its requirements. To shut out demands emanating beyond the self is precisely to suppress the conditions of significance, and hence to court trivialization. To the extent that people are seeking a moral ideal here, this self-immuring is self-stultifying; it destroys the condition in which the ideal can be realized.

Otherwise put, I can define my identity only against the background of things that matter. But to bracket out history, nature, society, the demands of solidarity, everything but what I find in myself, would be to eliminate all candidates for what matters. Only if I exist in a world in which history, or the demands of nature, or the needs of my fellow human beings, or the duties of citizenship, or the call of God, or something else of this order *matters* crucially, can

I define an identity for myself that is not trivial. Authenticity is not the enemy of demands that emanate from beyond the self; it supposes such demands.

But if this is so, there is something you can say to those who are enmired in the more trivialized modes of the culture of authenticity. Reason is not powerless. Of course, we haven't got very far here; just to showing that *some* self-transcending issues are indispensable [issue (b) above]. We have not shown that any particular *one* has to be taken seriously. The argument so far is just a sketch, and I hope to take it (just a little) further in subsequent sections. But for the moment I want to turn to the other issue, (a), whether there is something self-defeating in a mode of fulfilment that denies our ties to others.

V
THE NEED FOR RECOGNITION

(2) Another one of the common axes of criticism of the contemporary culture of authenticity is that it encourages a purely personal understanding of self-fulfilment, thus making the various associations and communities in which the person enters purely instrumental in their significance. At the broader social level, this is antithetical to any strong commitment to a community. In particular, it makes political citizenship, with its sense of duty and allegiance to political society, more and more marginal.[28] On the more intimate level, it fosters a view of relationships in which these ought to subserve personal fulfilment. The relationship is secondary to the self-realization of the partners. On this view, unconditional ties, meant to last for life, make little sense. A relationship may last till death, if it goes on

serving its purpose, but there is no point declaring a priori that it ought to.

This philosophy was articulated in a popular book of the mid-1970s: "You can't take everything with you when you leave on the midlife journey. You are moving away. Away from institutional claims and other people's agenda. Away from external valuations and accreditations. You are moving out of roles and into the self. If I could give everyone a gift for the send-off on this journey, it would be a tent. A tent for tentativeness. The gift of portable roots. . . . For each of us there is the opportunity to emerge reborn, *authentically* unique, with an enlarged capacity to love ourselves and embrace others. . . . The delights of self-discovery are always available. Though loved ones move in and out of our lives, the capacity to love remains."[29]

Authenticity seems once more to be defined here in a way that centres on the self, which distances us from our relations to others. And this has been seized on by the critics I quoted earlier. Can one say anything about this in reason?

Before sketching the direction of argument, it is important to see that the ideal of authenticity incorporates some notions of society, or at least of how people ought to live together. Authenticity is a facet of modern individualism, and it is a feature of all forms of individualism that they don't just emphasize the freedom of the individual but also propose models of society. We fail to see this when we confuse the two very different senses of individualism I distinguished earlier. The individualism of anomie and breakdown of course has no social ethic attached to it; but individualism as a moral principle or ideal must offer some view on how the individual should live with others.

So the great individualist philosophies also proposed models of society. Lockean individualism gave us the theory of society as contract. Later forms connected to notions of popular sovereignty. Two modes of social existence are quite evidently linked with the contemporary culture of self-fulfilment. The first is based on the notion of universal right: everyone should have the right and capacity to be themselves. This is what underlies soft relativism as a moral principle: no one has a right to criticize another's values. This inclines those imbued with this culture towards conceptions of procedural justice: the limit on anyone's self-fulfilment must be the safeguarding of an equal chance at this fulfilment for others.[30]

Secondly, this culture puts a great emphasis on relationships in the intimate sphere, especially love relationships. These are seen to be the prime loci of self-exploration and self-discovery and among the most important forms of self-fulfilment. This view reflects the continuation in modern culture of a trend that is now centuries old and that places the centre of gravity of the good life not in some higher sphere but in what I want to call "ordinary life," that is, the life of production and the family, of work and love.[31] Yet it also reflects something else that is important here: the acknowledgement that our identity requires recognition by others.

I wrote earlier of the way our identities are formed in dialogue with others, in agreement or struggle with their recognition of us. In a sense we can say that the discovery and articulation of this fact in its modern form came about in close connection with the developing ideal of authenticity.

We can distinguish two changes that have together made the modern preoccupation with identity and recognition inevitable. The first is the collapse of social hierarchies, which used to be the basis for honour. I am using "honour" in the ancien régime sense in which it is intrinsically linked to inequalities. For some to have honour in this sense it is essential that not everyone have it. This is the sense in which Montesquieu uses it in his description of monarchy. Honour is intrinsically a matter of "préférences."[32] It is also the sense we use when we speak of honouring someone, by giving her some public reward, say the Order of Canada. Plainly this would be without worth if tomorrow we decided to give it to every adult Canadian.

As against this notion of honour, we have the modern notion of dignity, now used in a universalist and egalitarian sense, where we talk of the inherent "dignity of human beings," or of citizen dignity. The underlying premiss here is that everyone shares in this.[33] This concept of dignity is the only one compatible with a democratic society, and it was inevitable that the old concept of honour be marginalized. But this has also meant that the forms of equal recognition have been essential to democratic culture. For instance, that everyone should be called Mister, Mrs, or Miss, rather than some people being called Lord or Lady, and others simply by their surnames, or, even more demeaning, by their first names, has been thought crucial in some democratic societies, such as the U.S.A. And more recently, for similar reasons, Mrs and Miss have been collapsed into Ms. Democracy has ushered in a politics of equal recognition, which has taken various forms over the years, and which now has returned in the form of demands for the equal status of cultures and of genders.

But the importance of recognition has been modified and intensified by the understanding of identity emerging with the ideal of authenticity. This was also in part an offshoot of the decline of hierarchical society. In those earlier societies, what we would now call a person's identity was largely fixed by his or her social position. That is, the background that made sense of what the person recognized as important was to a great extent determined by his or her place in society and whatever role or activities attached to this. The coming of a democratic society doesn't by itself do away with this, because people can still define themselves by their social roles. But what does decisively undermine this socially derived identification is the ideal of authenticity itself. As this emerges, for instance with Herder, it calls on me to discover my own original way of being. By definition, this cannot be socially derived but must be inwardly generated.

In the nature of the case, there is no such thing as inward generation, monologically understood, as I tried to argue above. My discovering my identity doesn't mean that I work it out in isolation but that I negotiate it through dialogue, partly overt, partly internalized, with others. That is why the development of an ideal of inwardly generated identity gives a new and crucial importance to recognition. My own identity crucially depends on my dialogical relations with others.

The point is not that this dependence on others arose with the age of authenticity. A form of dependence was always there. The socially derived identity was by its very nature dependent on society. But in the earlier age recognition never arose as a problem. Social recognition was built in to the socially derived identity from the very fact that it was based on social categories everyone took for granted. The thing about inwardly derived, personal, original identity is that it doesn't enjoy this recognition a priori. It has to win it through exchange, and it can fail. What has come about with the modern age is not the need for recognition but the conditions in which this can fail. And that is why the need is now *acknowledged* for the first time. In premodern times, people didn't speak of "identity" and "recognition," not because people didn't have (what we call) identities or because these didn't depend on recognition, but rather because these were then too unproblematic to be thematized as such.

It's not surprising that we can find some of the seminal ideas about citizen dignity and universal recognition, even if not in these terms, in Rousseau, one of the points of origin of the modern discourse of authenticity. Rousseau is a sharp critic of hierarchical honour, of "préférences." In a significant passage of the *Discourse on Inequality*, he pinpoints a fateful moment when society takes a turn towards corruption and injustice, when people begin to desire preferential esteem.[34] By contrast, in republican society, where all can share equally in the light of public attention, he sees the source of health.[35] But the topic of recognition is given its most influential early treatment in Hegel.[36]

The importance of recognition is now universally acknowledged in one form or another; on an intimate plane, we are all aware how identity can be formed or malformed in our contact with significant others. On the social plane, we have a continuing politics of equal recognition. Both have been shaped by the growing ideal of authenticity, and recognition plays an essential role in the culture that has arisen around it.

On the intimate level, we can see how much an original identity needs and is vulnerable to the recognition given or withheld by significant others. It is not surprising that in the culture of authenticity, relationships are seen as the key loci of self-discovery and self-confirmation. Love relationships are not important just because of the general emphasis in modern culture on the fulfilments of ordinary life. They are also crucial because they are the crucibles of inwardly generated identity.

On the social plane, the understanding that identities are formed in open dialogue, unshaped by a predefined social script, has made the politics of equal recognition more central and stressful. It has, in fact, considerably raised its stakes. Equal recognition is not just the appropriate mode for a healthy democratic society. Its refusal can inflict damage on those who are denied it, according to a widespread modern view. The projecting of an inferior or demeaning image on another can actually distort and oppress, to the extent that it is interiorized. Not only contemporary feminism but also race relations and discussions of multiculturalism are undergirded by the premiss that denied recognition can be a form of oppression. Whether this factor has been exaggerated may be questioned, but it is clear that the understanding of identity and authenticity has introduced a new dimension into the politics of equal recognition, which now operates with something like its own notion of authenticity, at least in so far as the denunciation of other-induced distortions are concerned.

In the light of this developing understanding of recognition over the last two centuries, we can see why the culture of authenticity has come to give precedence to the two modes of living together I mentioned earlier: (1) on the social level, the crucial principle is that of fairness, which demands equal chances for everyone to develop their own identity, which include — as we can now understand more clearly — the universal recognition of difference, in whatever modes this is relevant to identity, be it gender, racial, cultural, or to do with sexual orientation; and (2) in the intimate sphere, the identity-forming love relationship has a crucial importance.

The question with which I started this section can perhaps be put in this way: Can a mode of life that is centred on the self, in the sense that involves treating our associations as merely instrumental, be justified in the light of the ideal of authenticity? We can now perhaps rephrase it by asking whether these favoured modes of living together will allow of this kind of disaffiliated way of being.

(1) On the social level, it might seem that the answer is a clear yes. All the recognition of difference seems to require is that we accept some principle of procedural justice. It doesn't require that we acknowledge a strong allegiance to a citizen republic or any other form of political society. We can "hang loose," so long as we treat everyone equally. Indeed, it might even be argued that any political society based on some strong notion of the common good will of itself by this very fact endorse the lives of some people (those who support its notion of the common good) over others (those who seek other forms of good), and thereby deny equal recognition. Something like this, we saw, is the fundamental premiss of a liberalism of neutrality, which has many supporters today.

But this is too simple. Keeping in mind the argument of the previous section, we have to ask what is involved in truly recognizing difference. This means recognizing the equal value of different ways of being. It is this acknowledgement of equal value that a politics of identity-recognition requires. But what grounds the equality of value? We saw earlier that just the fact that people *choose* different ways of being doesn't make them equal; nor does the fact that they happen to *find themselves* in these different sexes, races, cultures. Mere difference can't itself be the ground of equal value.

If men and women are equal, it is not because they are different, but because overriding the difference are some properties, common or complementary, which are of value. They are beings capable of reason, or love, or memory, or dialogical recognition.

To come together on a mutual recognition of difference — that is, of the equal value of different identities — requires that we share more than a belief in this principle; we have to share also some standards of value on which the identities concerned check out as equal. There must be some substantive agreement on value, or else the formal principle of equality will be empty and a sham. We can pay lip-service to equal recognition, but we won't really share an understanding of equality unless we share something more. Recognizing difference, like self-choosing, requires a horizon of significance, in this case a shared one.

This doesn't show that we have to belong to a common political society; otherwise we couldn't recognize foreigners. And it doesn't by itself show that we have to take seriously the political society we are in. More needs to be filled in. But we can already see how the argument might go: how developing and nursing the commonalities of value between us become important, and one of the crucial ways we do this is sharing a participatory political life. The demands of recognizing difference themselves take us beyond mere procedural justice.

(2) How about our relationships? Can we see them as instrumental to our fulfilment, and thus as fundamentally tentative? Here the answer is easier. Surely not, if they are also going to form our identity. If the intense relations of self-exploration are going to be identity-forming, then they can't be in principle tentative — though they can, alas, in fact break up — and they can't be merely instrumental. Identities do in fact change, but we form them as the

identity of a person who has partly lived and will complete the living of a whole life. I don't define an identity for "me in 1991," but rather try to give meaning to my life as it has been and as I project it further on the basis of what it has been. My identity-defining relations can't be seen, in principle and in advance, as dispensable and destined for supersession. If my self-exploration takes the form of such serial and in principle temporary relationships, then it is not my identity that I am exploring, but some modality of enjoyment.

In the light of the ideal of authenticity, it would seem that having merely instrumental relationships is to act in a self-stultifying way. The notion that one can pursue one's fulfilment in this way seems illusory, in somewhat the same way as the idea that one can choose oneself without recognizing a horizon of significance beyond choice.

In any case, that's what this rather sketchy argument would suggest. I cannot claim to have established solid conclusions here, but I hope I have done something to suggest that the scope of rational argument is much greater than is often supposed, and therefore that this exploration of the sources of identity has some point.

VI
THE SLIDE TO SUBJECTIVISM

I have so far been suggesting a way of looking at what has been called "the culture of narcissism," the spread of an outlook that makes self-fulfilment the major value in life and that seems to recognize few external moral demands or serious commitments to others. The notion of self-fulfilment appears in these two respects very self-centred, hence the term "narcissism." I am saying that we should see this culture as reflecting in part an ethical aspiration, the ideal of authenticity, but one that doesn't itself license its self-centred modes. Rather, in the light of this ideal, these appear as deviant and trivialized modes.

This contrasts with two other common ways of looking at this culture. These see it either (a) as indeed powered by an ideal of self-fulfilment, but this ideal is understood as being just as self-centred as the practices that flow from it; or, (b) as just the expression of self-indulgence and egoism, that is, not actuated by an ideal at all. In practice, these two views tend to run into each other and become one, because the ideal supposed by (a) is so low and self-indulgent as to become virtually indistinguishable from (b).

Now (a) supposes in effect that when people propose a very self-centred form of self-fulfilment, they are quite impervious to the considerations of the previous two sections; either because their aspirations have nothing to do with the ideal of authenticity I have been tracing, or because people's moral views are independent of reason anyway. One can suppose them impervious either because one thinks of authenticity itself as a very low ideal, a rather thinly disguised appeal to self-indulgence; or because whatever the nature of contemporary ideals, one holds to a subjectivist view of moral convictions as mere projections that reason cannot alter.

Either way, both (a) and of course, a fortiori, (b), paint the culture of narcissism as quite at peace with itself, because on *any* reading it is exactly in theory what it is in practice. It meets its own aspirations and is thus impervious to argument. By contrast my view shows it to be full of tension, to be living an ideal that is not fully comprehended, and which properly understood would challenge many of its practices. Those who live it, sharing as they do our human condition, can be reminded of those features of our condition that show these practices to be questionable. The culture of narcissism lives an ideal that it is systematically falling below.

But if I'm right, then this fact needs explanation. Why does it fall below its ideal? What makes the ethic of authenticity prone to this kind of deviation into the trivial?

Of course, on one level, the motivation for adopting more self-centred forms can be clear enough. Our ties to others, as well as external moral demands, can easily be in conflict with our personal development. The demands of a career may be incompatible with obligations to our family, or with allegiance to some broader cause or principle. Life can seem easier if one can neglect these external constraints. Indeed, in certain contexts, where one is struggling to define a fragile and conflicted identity, forgetting the constraints can seem the only path to survival.

But moral conflicts of this kind have presumably always existed. What needs to be explained is the relatively greater ease with which these external constraints can now be dismissed or delegitimated. Where our ancestors on a similar path of self-assertion will have self-confessedly suffered from an unshakeable sense of wrongdoing, or at least of defiance of a legitimate order, many contemporaries come across as untroubled in their single-minded pursuit of self-development.

Part of the explanation lies in the social sphere. I mentioned above, in the second section, the accounts of modern culture that derive it from social change. While I think any simple one-way explanation can't hold water, it is clear that social change has had a great deal to do with the shape of modern culture. Certain ways of thinking and feeling may themselves facilitate social change, but when this comes about on a massive scale, it can entrench these ways and make them appear inescapable.

This is undoubtedly the case for the different forms of modern individualism. Individualist ideas developed in the thought and sensibility, particularly of educated Europeans, during the seventeenth century. These seem to have facilitated the growth of new political forms that challenged the ancient hierarchies, and of new modes of economic life, which gave a greater place to the market and to entrepreneurial enterprise. But once these new forms are in place, and people are brought up in them, then this individualism is greatly strengthened, because it is rooted in their everyday practice, in the way they make their living and the way they relate to others in political life. It comes to seem the only conceivable outlook, which it certainly wasn't for their ancestors who pioneered it.

This kind of entrenchment process can help explain the slide in the culture of authenticity. The self-centred forms are deviant, as we saw, in two respects. They tend to centre fulfilment on the individual, making his or her affiliations purely instrumental; they push, in other words, to a social *atomism*. And they tend to see fulfilment as just of the self, neglecting or delegitimating the demands that come from beyond our own desires or aspirations, be they from history, tradition, society, nature, or God; they foster, in other words, a radical anthropocentrism.

It is not hard to see how both of these stances come to be entrenched in modern industrial societies. From its very inception, this kind of society has involved mobility, at first of peasants off the land and to cities, and then across oceans and continents to new countries, and finally, today, from city to city following employment opportunities. Mobility is in a sense forced on us. Old ties are broken down. At the same time, city dwelling is transformed by the immense concentrations of population of the modern metropolis. By its very nature, this involves much more impersonal and casual contact, in place of the more intense, face-to-face relations in earlier times. All this cannot but generate a culture in which the outlook of social atomism becomes more and more entrenched.

In addition, our technocratic, bureaucratic society gives more and more importance to instrumental reason. This cannot but fortify atomism, because it induces us to see our communities, like so much else, in an instrumental perspective. But it also breeds anthropocentrism, in making us take an instrumental stance to all facets of our life and surroundings: to the past, to nature, as well as to our social arrangements.

So part of the explanation for the deviancy in the culture of authenticity is to be traced to the fact that this is being lived in an industrial-technological-bureaucratic society. In fact, the hold of instrumental reason is evident in a host of ways in various facets of the human-potential movement, whose dominant purpose is intended to be self-fulfilment. Very often we are offered techniques, based on supposed scientific findings, to achieve psychic integration or peace of mind. The dream of the quick fix is present here too, as elsewhere, in spite of the fact that from the very beginning, and still today, the goal of self-fulfilment has been understood as antithetical to that of mere instrumental control. A quick-fix technique for letting go is the ultimate contradiction.

But the social setting doesn't provide the whole story. There are also reasons internal to the ideal of authenticity that facilitate the slide. In fact, there has not just been one slide; there have been two, which have had complex, criss-crossing relations.

The first is the one I have been talking about, the slide towards self-centred modes of the ideal of self-fulfilment in the popular culture of our time. The second is a movement of "high" culture, towards a kind of nihilism, a negation of all horizons of significance, which has been proceeding now for a century and a half. The major figure here is Nietzsche (although he used the term "nihilism" in a different sense, to designate something he rejected), though the roots of the twentieth-century forms are also to be found in the image of the "poète maudit" and in Baudelaire. Aspects of this line of thinking found expression in some strands of modernism, and it has emerged among writers who are often referred to today as postmodern, such as Jacques Derrida or the late Michel Foucault.

The impact of these thinkers is paradoxical. They carry their Nietzschean challenge to our ordinary categories to the point even of "deconstructing" the ideal of authenticity, and the very notion of the self. But in fact, the Nietzschean critique of all "values" as created cannot but exalt and entrench anthropocentrism. In the end, it leaves the agent, even with all his or her doubts about the category of the "self," with a sense of untrammelled power and freedom before a world that imposes no standards, ready to enjoy "free play,"[37] or to indulge in an aesthetics of the self.[38] As this "higher" theory filters down into the popular culture of authenticity — we can see this, for instance, among students, who are at the juncture of the two cultures — it further strengthens the self-centred modes, gives them a certain patina of deeper philosophical justification.

And yet all this emerges, I want to claim, from the same sources as the ideal of authenticity. How could this be? Michel Foucault's invocation of the aesthetic in a late interview points us in the right direction. But to make the links here intelligible, we have to bring in the expressive aspects of modern individualism.

The notion that each one of us has an original way of being human entails that each of us has to discover what it is to be ourselves. But the discovery can't be made by consulting pre-existing models, by hypothesis. So it can be made only by articulating it afresh. We discover what we have it in us to be by becoming that mode of life, by giving expression in our speech and action to what is original in us. The notion that revelation comes through expression is what I want to capture in speaking of the "expressivism" of the modern notion of the individual.[39]

This suggests right away a close analogy, even a connection, between self-discovery and artistic creation. With Herder, and the expressivist understanding of human life, the relation becomes very intimate. Artistic creation becomes the paradigm mode in which people can come to self-definition. The artist becomes in some way the paradigm case of the human being, as agent of original self-definition. Since about 1800, there has been a tendency to heroize the artist, to see in his or her life the essence of the human condition, and to venerate him or her as a seer, the creator of cultural values.

But of course, along with this has gone a new understanding of art. No longer defined mainly by imitation, by *mimēsis* of reality, art is understood now more in terms of creation. These two ideas go together. If we become ourselves by expressing what we're about, and if what we become is by hypothesis original, not based on the pre-existing, then what we express is not an imitation of the pre-existing either, but a new creation. We think of the imagination as creative.

Let's look a bit closer at this case, which has become a paradigm for us, where I discover myself through my work as an artist, through what I create. My self-discovery passes through a creation, the making of something original and new. I forge a new artistic language — new way of painting, new metre or form of poetry, new way of writing a novel — and through this and this alone I become what I have it in me to be. Self-discovery requires *poiēsis*, making. That will play a crucial role in one of the directions this idea of authenticity has evolved in.

But before looking at this, I want to note the close relation between our ordinary ideas of self-discovery and the work of the creative artist. Self-discovery involves the imagination, like art. We think of people who have achieved originality in their lives as "creative." And that we describe the lives of non-artists in artistic terms matches our tendency to consider artists as somehow paradigm achievers of self definition.

But there is another range of reasons for this close drawing together of art and self-definition. It's not just that both involve creative *poiēsis*. It is also that self-definition comes early to be contrasted to morality. Some theories hold them tightly together. Rousseau does, for instance: "le sentiment de l'existence" would make me a perfectly moral creature if I were but in full contact with it. But very early on it came to be seen that this was not necessarily so. The demands of self-truth, contact with self, harmony within ourselves could be quite different from the demands of right treatment that we were expected to accord to others. Indeed, the very idea of originality, and the associated notion that the enemy of authenticity can be social conformity, forces on us the idea that authenticity will have to struggle against *some* externally imposed rules. We can, of course, believe that it will be in harmony with the *right* rules, but it is at least clear that there is a notional difference between these two kinds of demand, that of truth to self and those of intersubjective justice.

This emerges more and more clearly in the recognition that the demands of authenticity are closely bound up with the aesthetic. We are very familiar with this term, and we think that the aesthetic has always been a category for people, at any rate, for as long as they have loved art and beauty. But that isn't so. The notion of the aesthetic emerges out of another parallel change in the eighteenth century in the understanding of art, connected with the shift of models from imitation to creativity.

Where art is understood as primarily a kind of imitation of reality, it can be defined in terms of the reality portrayed, or its manner of portrayal. But the eighteenth century sees another one of those shifts towards the subject, parallel to the one I described earlier in connection with the philosophy of the moral sense. The specificity of art and beauty cease to be defined in terms of the reality or its manner of depiction, and come to be identified by the kinds of feeling they arouse in us, a feeling of its own special kind, different from the moral and other kinds of pleasure. Once more, it is Hutcheson, drawing on Shaftesbury, who is one of the pioneers in this line of thought, but by the end of the century it is made famous, almost canonical, through the formulation given it by Immanuel Kant.

For Kant, following Shaftesbury, beauty involves a sense of satisfaction, but one that is distinct from the fulfilment of any desire, or even from the satisfaction accruing to moral excellence. It is a satisfaction for itself, as it were. Beauty gives its own intrinsic fulfilment. Its goal is internal.

But authenticity too comes to be understood in parallel fashion, as its own goal. It is born, as I described it above, out of a shift in the centre of gravity of the moral demand on us: self-truth and self-wholeness are seen more and more not as means to be moral, as independently defined, but as something valuable for their own sake. Self-wholeness and the aesthetic are ready to be brought together, a unity to which Schiller gave an immensely influential expression in his *Letters on the Aesthetic Education of Man*.[40] For Schiller, the enjoyment of beauty gives us a unity and wholeness beyond the divisions that arise in us from the struggle between morality and desire. This wholeness is something different from the achievement of morality, and in the end Schiller seems to be implying that it is higher, because it engages us totally in a way that morality cannot. Of course, for Schiller, the two are still compatible, they dovetail. But they are ready to be contrasted, because the aesthetic wholeness is an independent goal, with its own *telos*, its own form of goodness and satisfaction.

All this contributes to the close links between authenticity and art. And this helps explain some of the developments of the notion of authenticity in the last two centuries; in particular, the development of forms in which the demands of authenticity have been pitched against those of morality. Authenticity involves originality, it demands a revolt against convention. It is easy to see how standard morality itself can come to be seen as inseparable from stifling convention. Morality as normally understood obviously involves crushing much that is elemental and instinctive in us, many of our deepest and most powerful desires. So there develops a branch of the search for authenticity that pits it against the moral. Nietzsche, who seeks a kind of self-making in the register of the aesthetic, sees this as quite incompatible with the traditional Christian-inspired ethic of benevolence. And he has been followed and exceeded by various attempts to champion the instinctual depths, even violence, against the "bourgeois" ethic of order. Influential examples in our century are, in their very different ways: Marinetti and the Futurists, Antonin Artaud and his Theatre of Cruelty, and Georges Bataille. The cult of violence was also one of the roots of Fascism.

So authenticity can develop in many branches. Are they all equally legitimate? I don't think so. I am not trying to say that these apostles of evil are simply wrong. They may be on to something, some strain within the very idea of authenticity, that may pull us in more than one direction. But I think that the popular "postmodern" variants of our day, which have attempted to delegitimate horizons of significance, as we see with Derrida, Foucault, and their followers, are indeed proposing deviant forms. The deviancy takes the form of forgetting about one whole set of demands on authenticity while focussing exclusively on another.

Briefly, we can say that authenticity (A) involves (i) creation and construction as well as discovery, (ii) originality, and frequently (iii) opposition to the rules of society and even potentially to what we recognize as morality. But it is also true, as we saw, that it (B) requires (i) openness to horizons of significance (for otherwise the creation loses the background that can save it from insignificance) and (ii) a self-definition in dialogue. That these demands may be in tension has to be allowed. But what must be wrong is a simple privileging of one over the other, of (A), say, at the expense of (B), or vice versa.

This is what the trendy doctrines of "deconstruction" involve today. They stress (A.i), the constructive, creative nature of our expressive languages, while altogether forgetting (B.i). And they capture the extremer forms of (A.iii), the amoralism of creativity, while forgetting (B.ii), its dialogical setting, which binds us to others.

There is something incoherent about this, because these thinkers buy into the background outlook of authenticity, for instance in their understanding of the creative, self-constitutive powers of language. This is something the more disengaged, scientistic philosophy of human life cannot accept. But they want to buy into it while ignoring some of its essential constituents.

However, whether right or not, we can see how strong the temptation can be to espouse this kind of theory. It is implicit in the strains within the ideal of authenticity itself between the sides I've identified as (A) and (B). And once one does rush off in this direction, exalting (A) over (B), something else comes into play. The understanding of value as created gives a sense of freedom and power. The fascination with violence in the twentieth century has been a love affair with power. But even in milder forms, neo-Nietzschean theories generate a sense of radical freedom.

This connects up with that other idea, which as I have said has been closely connected with authenticity since the beginning, self-determining freedom. Their relations have been complex, involving both affinity and contestation.

The affinity is obvious. Authenticity is itself an idea of freedom; it involves my finding the design of my

life myself, against the demands of external conformity. The basis is there for an alliance. But this is just
what makes the differences all the more fateful.
Because the notion of self-determining freedom,
pushed to its limit, doesn't recognize any bound-
aries, anything given that I *have* to respect in my
exercise of self-determining choice. It can easily tip
over into the most extreme forms of anthropocentrism. It has, of course, a social variant, formulated in
Rousseau's *Social Contract* and developed in their own
ways by Marx and Lenin, which certainly ties the
individual to society. But at the same time, these variants have pushed human-centredness to new heights,
in their atheism, and in their ecological aggressive-
ness, which has surpassed even that of capitalist
society.[41]

In the end, authenticity can't, shouldn't, go all the
way with self-determining freedom. It undercuts
itself. Yet the temptation is understandably there.
And where the tradition of authenticity falls for any
other reason into anthropocentrism, the alliance easily recommends itself, becomes almost irresistible.
That's because anthropocentrism, by abolishing all
horizons of significance, threatens us with a loss of
meaning and hence a trivialization of our predicament. At one moment, we understand our situation
as one of high tragedy, alone in a silent universe,
without intrinsic meaning, condemned to create
value. But at a later moment, the same doctrine, by
its own inherent bent, yields a flattened world, in
which there aren't very meaningful choices because
there aren't any crucial issues. The fate of the great
"postmodern" doctrines that I've been describing

here, as they impact on the North American university, illustrates this. They become both flatter and kinder than the originals. Flatter, because they serve in the end to bolster the more self-centred images of authenticity. Kinder, because they are taken as supports for the demands to recognize difference. Foucault, in the American university, is emphatically seen in general as a figure of the left. This is not necessarily the case in France, and even less in Germany.[42]

In a flattened world, where the horizons of meaning becomer fainter, the ideal of self-determining freedom comes to exercise a more powerful attraction. It seems that significance can be conferred by *choice*, by making my life an exercise in freedom, even when all other sources fail. Self-determining freedom is in part the default solution of the culture of authenticity, while at the same time it is its bane, since it further intensifies anthropocentrism. This sets up a vicious circle that heads us towards a point where our major remaining value is choice itself. But this, as we saw above, deeply subverts both the ideal of authenticity and the associated ethic of recognizing difference.

These are the strains and weaknesses within the culture of authenticity, which along with the pressures of an atomizing society precipitate it on its slide.

VII
LA LOTTA CONTINUA

I've been painting a portrait of the culture of authenticity as actuated, even in its most "narcissistic" variants, by an ideal of authenticity, which properly understood condemns these variants. It is a culture that suffers from a constitutive tension. This is in contrast with the common view of the more self-centred forms of self-fulfilment as merely a product of self-indulgent egoism, or at best as actuated by an ideal no better than the least admirable practices.

Why hold my view? Well, the first reason is that it seems to me true. This ideal does seem to me still operative in our culture, and the tension seems to be there. But what are the consequences for our action if my view is true? Seeing things the way I'm proposing leads to a quite different stance towards this culture. One common stance today, especially among such critics as Bloom, Bell, and Lasch, is to look askance at the goal of self-fulfilment as somehow tainted with egoism. This can easily lead to a blanket condemnation of the culture of authenticity. On the other hand, there are those who are very much "into" this culture, for whom everything is all right as it is. The picture suggested here leads to neither of the above. It suggests that we undertake a work of retrieval, that we identify and articulate the higher ideal behind the more or less debased practices, and then criticize these practices from the standpoint of their own motivating ideal. In other words, instead of dismissing this culture altogether, or just endorsing it as it is, we ought to attempt to raise its practice by making more palpable to its participants what the ethic they subscribe to really involves.

This means engaging in a work of persuasion. This seems neither possible nor desirable, if you take either of the other standpoints, but it is the only appropriate policy on the view I've been defending. Any cultural field involves a struggle; people with different and incompatible views contend, criticize, and condemn each other. There is already a battle going on between the boosters and the knockers as far as the culture of authenticity is concerned. I'm suggesting that this struggle is a mistake; *both* sides are wrong. What we ought to be doing is fighting over the meaning of authenticity, and from the standpoint developed here, we ought to be trying to persuade people that self-fulfilment, so far from excluding unconditional relationships and moral demands beyond the self, actually requires these in some form. The struggle ought not to be *over* authenticity, for or against, but *about* it, defining its proper meaning. We ought to be trying to lift the culture back up, closer to its motivating ideal.

Of course, all this assumes three things: the three premisses that I laid out at the end of Section II: (1) that authenticity is truly an ideal worth espousing; (2) that you can establish in reason what it involves; and (3) that this kind of argument can make a difference in practice — that is, you can't believe that people are so locked in by the various social developments that condition them to, say, atomism and instrumental reason that they couldn't change their ways no matter how persuasive you were.

I hope I have done something in the preceding sections to make (2) plausible. Even if I haven't produced any unanswerable arguments, I hope I have shown to some extent how arguments can be developed in this area that could convince us. As to (3), while everyone must recognize how powerfully we are conditioned by our industrial technological civilization, those views that portray us as totally locked in and unable to change our behaviour short of smashing the whole "system" have always seemed to me wildly exaggerated. But I want to say more about this in the next section. For the present let me just say a few words about (1), the worth of this ideal.

I don't have a lot fresh to say on this either, at this point. Because it seems to me that the ideal, as we understand it out of its richest sources, speaks for itself. I will just state baldly what I believe does emerge out of a full account from these sources (fuller than I've been able to offer here).[43]

I believe that in articulating this ideal over the last two centuries, Western culture has identified one of the important potentialities of human life. Like other facets of modern individualism — for instance, that which calls on us to work out our own opinions and beliefs for ourselves — authenticity points us towards a more self-responsible form of life. It allows us to live (potentially) a fuller and more differentiated life, because more fully appropriated as our own. There are dangers — we've been exploring some of them. When we succumb to these, it may be that we fall in some respects below what we would have been had this culture never developed. But at its best authenticity allows a richer mode of existence.

But beyond this, I would like to make an ad hominem point. I think that everybody in our culture feels the force of this ideal, even those I have been identifying as "knockers": people who think that the whole language of self-fulfilment and finding one's own path is suspect and either nonsense or a vehicle of self-indulgence. People who think it's nonsense generally have a hard-line, scientistic attitude to the world. They think human beings should be understood as much as possible in the language of science, and they take the natural sciences as their model. So talk of self-fulfilment or authenticity can seem to them vague and woolly. Other critics, like Allan Bloom, are humanists. They don't share this reductive, scientistic view, but they seem to understand this language as an expression of moral laxity, or at least as reflecting simply a loss of the more stringent ideals formerly dominant in our culture.

And yet it is hard to find anyone we would consider as being in the mainstream of our Western societies who, faced with their own life choices, about career or relationships, gives no weight at all to something they would identify as fulfilment, or self-development, or realizing their potential, or for which they would find some other term from the range that has served to articulate this ideal. They may override these considerations in the name of other goods, but they feel their force. There are of course immigrants from other cultures, and people who still live in very traditional enclaves, but we can practically *define* the cultural mainstream of Western liberal society in terms of those who feel the draw of this and the other main forms of individualism. This is, indeed, very often the source of difficult and painful intergenerational battles in immigrant families, just because these individualisms define the mainstream into which the children are being unavoidably acculturated.

This is, admittedly, not an argument for the *worth* of the ideal. But it ought to induce some humility in its opponents. Would it make sense to try to root it out? Or does the policy recommended here make more sense in *our* situation, namely, espousing the ideal at its best, and trying to raise our practice up to this level?

So my interpretation grounds a rather different practice. It sends us off in a different direction from the other two. But it also offers a quite different perspective on things. It does indeed appear that the more self-centred forms of fulfilment have been gaining ground in recent decades. This is what has caused the alarm. People do seem to be seeing their relationships as more revocable. Rises in the rate of divorce give only a partial indication of the increase in break-ups, because of the large number of unmarried couples in our society. More people seem less rooted in their communities of origin, and there seems to be a fall-off in citizen participation.

Now if you think that this represents a new set of values that today's rising generation has unproblematically plumped for — or even more, if you think they have plumped for an abandonment of traditional ties in favour of sheer egoism — then you will despair for the future. There doesn't seem much reason why the trend should be reversed. Your despair will be intensified to the extent that you attribute the change to the social factors I mentioned earlier: like increased mobility, and our increasing involvement in jobs or social situations that involve our acting instrumentally, even manipulatively, towards the people around us. Because these trends seem destined to continue, in some cases even to intensify. And so the future appears to promise only ever-increasing levels of narcissism.

The perspective is different if you see these developments in the light of the ethic of authenticity. For then they don't just represent a shift in value that is unproblematic for the people concerned. Rather, you see the new, self-centred practices as the site of an ineradicable tension. The tension comes from the sense of an ideal that is not being fully met in reality.

And this tension can turn into a struggle, where people try to articulate the shortfall of practice, and criticize it.

On this perspective, society isn't simply moving in one direction. The fact that there is tension and struggle means that it can go either way. On one side are all the factors, social and internal, that drag the culture of authenticity down to its most self-centred forms; on the other are the inherent thrust and requirements of this ideal. A battle is joined, which can go back and forth.

This may come across as good news or bad news. It will be bad news for anyone who hoped for a definitive solution. We can never return to the age before these self-centred modes could tempt and solicit people. Like all forms of individualism and freedom, authenticity opens an age of responsibilization, if I can use this term. By the very fact that this culture develops, people are made more self-responsible. It is in the nature of this kind of increase of freedom that people can sink lower, as well as rise higher. Nothing will ever ensure a systematic and irreversible move to the heights.

This was the dream of various revolutionary movements, for instance of Marxism. Once one abolished capitalism, only the great and admirable fruits of modern freedom would flower; the abuses and deviant forms would wither away. But that's not how it can ever be in a free society, which at one and the same time will give us the highest forms of self-responsible moral initiative and dedication and, say, the worst forms of pornography. The claim of erstwhile Marxist societies that pornography was simply a reflection of capitalism has now been shown up for the hollow boast it was.

And so this can come across as good news as well. If the best can never be definitively guaranteed, then nor are decline and triviality inevitable. The nature of a free society is that it will always be the locus of a struggle between higher and lower forms of freedom. Neither side can abolish the other, but the line can be moved, never definitively but at least for some people for some time, one way or the other. Through social action, political change, and winning hearts and minds, the better forms can gain ground, at least for a while. In a sense, a genuinely free society can take as its self-description the slogan put forward in quite another sense by revolutionary movements like the Italian Red Brigades: "la lotta continua," the struggle goes on — in fact, forever.

The perspective I'm proposing thus breaks quite definitively with the cultural pessimism that has grown in recent decades and that books like Bloom's and Bell's feed. The analogy for our age is not the decline of the Roman empire, as decadence and a slide into hedonism make us incapable of maintaining our political civilization. This is not to say that *some* societies may not slip badly into alienation and bureaucratic rigidity. And some may indeed lose their quasi-imperial status. The fact that the United States is in danger of suffering both these negative changes has perhaps understandably increased the hold of cultural pessimism there.[44] But the United States is not the Western world, and perhaps even it should not be taken as a single entity, because it is an immensely varied society, made up of very different milieux and groups. Of course, there will be gains and losses, but overall "la lotta continua."

Almost needless to say, I'm not proposing the mirror-image view either, a cultural optimism of the kind popular in the 1960s, such as in Charles Reich's *The Greening of America*, which saw the rise of a spontaneous, gentle, loving, and ecologically responsible culture. This dream rises as naturally from the distorted perspective of the boosters as the pessimistic one does from that of the knockers. I want to stay away from both these views, not in a middle ground so much as on a completely different ground. I suggest that in this matter we look not for the Trend, whatever it is, up or down, but that we break with our temptation to discern irreversible trends, and see that there is a struggle here, whose outcome is continually up for grabs.

But if I am right, and the struggle is as I describe it, then the cultural pessimism of the knockers is not only mistaken, it is also counter-productive. Because root-and-branch condemnation of the culture of authenticity as illusion or narcissism is not a way to move us closer to the heights. As it is, an alliance of people with a disengaged scientistic outlook, and those with more traditional ethical views, as well as some proponents of an outraged high culture, unite to condemn this culture. But this cannot help. A way that might help change the people engaged in this culture (and at some level, this includes everyone, even the critics, I want to claim) would be to enter sympathetically into its animating ideal and to try to show what it really requires. But when the ideal is by implication condemned and ridiculed along with existing practice, attitudes harden. The critics are written off as pure reactionaries, and no reassessment takes place.

In the resulting polarization between boosters and knockers, what precisely gets lost is a rich understanding of this ideal. Both in a sense conspire to identify it with its lowest, most self-centred expressions. It is against this conspiracy that the work of retrieval has to be done, which I have in a sense been sketching in the foregoing sections.

VIII
SUBTLER LANGUAGES

*A*long with the ideal, a very important distinction gets fudged over in this polarized debate, one that is essential for understanding modern culture. In a sense, this culture has seen a many-faceted movement that one could call "subjectivation": that is, things centre more and more on the subject, and in a host of ways. Things that were once settled by some external reality — traditional law, say, or nature — are now referred to our choice. Issues where we were meant to accept the dictates of authority we now have to think out for ourselves. Modern freedom and autonomy centres us on ourselves, and the ideal of authenticity requires that we discover and articulate our own identity.

But there are two importantly different facets to this movement, one concerning the *manner* and the other concerning the *matter* or *content* of action. We can illustrate this with the ideal of authenticity. On one level, it clearly concerns the *manner* of espousing any end or form of life. Authenticity is clearly self-referential: this has to be *my* orientation. But this doesn't mean that on another level the *content* must be self-referential: that my goals must express or fulfil my desires or aspirations, *as against* something that stands beyond these. I can find fulfilment in God, or a political cause, or tending the earth. Indeed, the argument above suggests that we will find genuine fulfilment only in something like this, which has significance independent of us or our desires.

To confuse these two kinds of self-referentiality is catastrophic. It closes off the way ahead, which can't involve going back behind the age of authenticity. Self-referentiality of manner is unavoidable in our culture. To confuse the two is to create the illusion that self-referentiality of matter is equally inescapable. The confusion lends legitimacy to the worst forms of subjectivism.

The development of modern art gives us a good example of how these two kinds of subjectivation are crucially different and yet how easily they are confused. Since art is also a crucial terrain for the ideal of authenticity, as we have seen, this is especially worth exploring here.

The change I want to talk about here goes back to the end of the eighteenth century and is related to the shift from an understanding of art as *mimēsis* to one that stresses creation, which I discussed in section VI. It concerns what one might call the languages of art, that is, the publicly available reference points that, say, poets and painters can draw on. As Shakespeare could draw on the correspondences, for instance when, to make us feel the full horror of the act of regicide, he has a servant report the "unnatural" events that have been evoked in sympathy with this terrible deed: the night in which Duncan is murdered is an unruly one, with "lamentings heard i' the air; strange screams of death," and it remains dark even though the day should have started. On the previous Tuesday a falcon had been killed by a mousing owl, and Duncan's horses turned wild in the night, "Contending 'gainst obedience, as they would / Make war with mankind." In a similar way, painting could long draw on the publicly understood subjects of divine and secular history, events, and personages that had heightened meaning, as it were, built in to them, like the Madonna and Child or the oath of the Horatii.

But for a couple of centuries now we have been living in a world in which these points of reference no longer hold for us. No one now believes the doctrine of the correspondences, as this was accepted in the Renaissance, and neither divine nor secular history has a generally accepted significance. It is not that one cannot write a poem about the correspondences. Baudelaire did. It is rather that this can't draw on the simple acceptance of the formerly public doctrines. The poet himself didn't subscribe to them in their canonical form. He is getting at something different, some personal vision he is trying to triangulate to through this historical reference, the "forest of symbols" that he sees in the world around him. But to grasp this forest, we need to understand not so much the erstwhile public doctrine (about which no one remembers any details anyway) but, as we might put it, the way it resonates in the poet's sensibility.

To take another example, Rilke speaks of angels. But his angels are not to be understood by their place in the traditionally defined order. Rather, we have to triangulate to the meaning of this term through the whole range of images with which Rilke articulates his sense of things. "Who if I cried out would hear me among the orders of angels?", begin the *Duino Elegies*. Their being beyond these cries partly defines these angels. We cannot get at them through a medieval treatise on the ranks of cherubim and seraphim, but we have to pass through this articulation of Rilke's sensibility.

We could describe the change in this way: where formerly poetic language could rely on certain publicly available orders of meaning, it now has to consist in a language of articulated sensibility. Earl Wasserman has shown how the decline of the old order with its established background of meanings made necessary the development of new poetic languages in the Romantic period. Pope, for instance, in his *Windsor Forest*, could draw on age-old views of the order of nature as a commonly available source of poetic images. For Shelley, this resource is no longer available; the poet must articulate his own world of references, and make them believable. As Wasserman explains it, "Until the end of the eighteenth century there was sufficient intellectual homogeneity for men to share certain assumptions . . .

In varying degrees . . . man accepted . . . the Christian interpretation of history, the sacramentalism of nature, the Great Chain of Being, the analogy of the various planes of creation, the conception of man as microcosm . . . These were cosmic syntaxes in the public domain; and the poet could afford to think of his art as imitative of 'nature' since these patterns were what he meant by 'nature'.

"By the nineteenth century these world-pictures had passed from consciousness . . . The change from a mimetic to a creative conception of poetry is not merely a critical philosophical phenomenon . . . Now . . . an additional formulative act was required of the poet . . . Within itself the modern poem must both formulate its own cosmic syntax and shape the autonomous poetic reality that the cosmic syntax permits; 'nature', which was once prior to the poem and available for imitation, now shares with the poem a common origin in the poet's creativity."[45]

The Romantic poets and their successors have to articulate an original vision of the cosmos. When Wordsworth and Hölderlin describe the natural world around us, in *The Prelude*, *The Rhine*, or *Homecoming*, they no longer play on an established gamut of references, as Pope could still do in *Windsor Forest*. They make us aware of something in nature for which there are as yet no adequate words.[46] The poems are finding the words for us. In this "subtler language" — the term is borrowed from Shelley — something is defined and created as well as manifested. A watershed has been passed in the history of literature.

Something similar happens in painting in the

early nineteenth century. Caspar David Friedrich, for instance, distances himself from the traditional iconography. He is searching for a symbolism in nature that is not based on the accepted conventions. The ambition is to let "the forms of nature speak directly, their power released by their ordering within the work of art."[47] Friedrich too is seeking a subtler language; he is trying to say something for which no adequate terms exist and whose meaning has to be sought in his works rather than in a pre-existing lexicon of references.[48] He builds on the late-eighteenth-century sense of the affinity between our feelings and natural scenes, but in an attempt to articulate more than a subjective reaction. "Feeling can never be contrary to nature, is always consistent with nature."[49]

This represents a qualitative change in artistic languages. That is, it is not just a question of fragmentation. We couldn't describe it by just saying that formerly poets had a commonly acknowledged language and now every one has his or her own. This makes it sound as though, if we could just agree, we could give, say, Rilke's vision of order the same status of a public language that the old Chain of Being enjoyed.

But the change is more far-reaching than that. What could never be recovered is the public understanding that angels are part of a human-independent ontic order, having their angelic natures quite independently of human articulation, and hence accessible through languages of description (theology, philosophy) that are not at all those of articulated sensibility. By contrast, Rilke's "order" can become ours only through being ratified afresh in the sensibility of each new reader. In these circumstances, the very idea that one such order should be embraced to the exclusion of all the others — a demand that is virtually inescapable in the traditional context — ceases to have any force. It is only too clear how another sensibility, another context of images, might give us a quite different take, even on what we might nevertheless see as a similar vision of reality.

So contemporary "angels" have to be human-related, one might say language-related, in a way their forebears were not. They cannot be separated from a certain language of articulation, which is, as it were, their home element. And this language in turn is rooted in the personal sensibility of the poet, and understood only by those whose sensibility resonates like the poet's.

Perhaps the contrast can be seen most starkly if we think of how we can also call on individual intuitions to map a public domain of references. Linguistics may make use of our linguistic intuitions of grammaticality. To make these available usually requires a reflexive turn. I ask myself: Can you say "She don't got a cent"? and I answer negatively. But there is no call to talk here of "personal vision." What I am mapping is precisely a piece of the publicly available background, what we all lean on and count with while we communicate. By contrast, what Eliot or Pound or Proust invites me to has an ineradicably personal dimension.

In terms of the earlier discussion, this means that an important subjectivation has taken place in post-

Romantic art. But it is clearly a subjectivation of *manner*. It concerns how the poet has access to whatever he or she is pointing us to. It by no means follows that there has to be a subjectivation of *matter*, that is, that post-Romantic poetry must be in some sense exclusively an expression of the self. This is a common view, which seems to be given some credence by well-known phrases like Wordsworth's description of poetry as "the spontaneous overflow of powerful feeling." But Wordsworth himself was trying to do more than articulate his own feelings when he wrote in "Tintern Abbey" of

A presence that disturbs me with the joy
Of elevated thoughts; a sense sublime
Of something far more deeply interfused,
Whose dwelling is the light of setting suns,
And the round ocean and the living air,
And the blue sky, and in the mind of man:
A motion and a spirit, that impels
All thinking things, all objects of all thought,
And rolls through all things. (*ll.*94–102)

And the effort of some of the best of modern poets has been precisely to articulate something beyond the self. We need only think of Rilke in his "Neue Gedichte," and of a poem like "The Panther," where he tries to articulate the things from within themselves, as it were.

The confusion of matter and manner is easy to make, just because modern poetry cannot be the exploration of an "objective" order in the classical sense of a publicly accessible domain of references. And the confusion lies not only with commentators.

It is easy enough to conclude that the decline of the classical order leaves only the self to celebrate, and its powers. The slide to subjectivism, and its blend of authenticity with self-determining freedom, is all too readily open. A great deal of modern art just turns on the celebration of human powers and feelings. The Futurists again come to mind as examples.

But some of the very greatest of twentieth-century writers are not subjectivist in this sense. Their agenda is not the self, but something beyond. Rilke, Eliot, Pound, Joyce, Mann, and others are among them. Their example shows that the inescapable rooting of poetic language in personal sensibility doesn't have to mean that the poet no longer explores an order beyond the self. In his *Duino Elegies*, for instance, Rilke is trying to tell us something about our predicament, about the relation of the living to the dead, about human frailty, and the power of transfiguration present in language.

So the two kinds of subjectivation have to be distinguished if we are to understand modern art. And this distinction has great relevance to the ongoing cultural struggle I referred to earlier. For some of the important issues of our time, concerning love and our place in the natural order, need to be explored in such languages of personal resonance. To take a salient example, just because we no longer believe in the doctrines of the Great Chain of Being, we don't need to see ourselves as set in a universe that we can consider simply as a source of raw materials for our projects. We may still need to see ourselves as part of a larger order that can make claims on us.

Indeed, this latter may be thought of as urgent. It would greatly help to stave off ecological disaster if we could recover a sense of the demand that our natural surroundings and wilderness make on us. The subjectivist bias that both instrumental reason and the ideologies of self-centred fulfilment make dominant in our time renders it almost impossible to state the case here. Albert Borgman points out how much of the argument for ecological restraint and responsibility is couched in anthropocentric language.[50] Restraint is shown as necessary for human welfare. This is true and important enough, but it is not the whole story. Nor does it capture the full extent of our intuitions here, which often point us to a sense that nature and our world make a claim on us.

But we cannot explore these intuitions effectively without the help that our languages of personal resonance can give us. That is why the failure to recognize that these can be used non-subjectivistically — the confusion of the two kinds of subjectivation — can have important moral consequences. Proponents of disengaged reason or of subjective fulfilment may embrace these consequences gladly. For them, there is nothing there beyond the self to explore. Root-and-branch critics of modernity hanker after the old public orders, and they assimilate personally resonating visions to mere subjectivism. Some stern moralists, too, want to contain this murky area of the personal, and tend as well to block together all its manifestations, whether subjectivist or exploratory. We recognize here the familiar coalition that conspires unwittingly to sustain a low and trivialized view of the ethic of authenticity.

But in blocking out this kind of exploration beyond the self, they are also depriving us of one of our main weapons in the continuing struggle against the flattened and trivialized forms of modern culture. They are closing off the kind of exploration that could make certain demands from beyond the self more palpable and real for us — for instance, those that underlie a more-than-anthropocentric ecological policy. We can see again how the perspective of the polarized debate between boosters and knockers, between cultural optimism and pessimism, can be crippling when it comes to engaging in the real, never-completed battle to realize the highest potentialities of our modern culture.

If authenticity is being true to ourselves, is recovering our own "sentiment de l'existence," then perhaps we can only achieve it integrally if we recognize that this sentiment connects us to a wider whole. It was perhaps not an accident that in the Romantic period the self-feeling and the feeling of belonging to nature were linked.[51] Perhaps the loss of a sense of belonging through a publicly defined order needs to be compensated by a stronger, more inner sense of linkage. Perhaps this is what a great deal of modern poetry has been trying to articulate; and perhaps we need few things more today than such articulation.

IX
AN IRON CAGE?

I have been discussing at length the first of the three worries about modernity that I outlined in the first section. I haven't got much time to address the other two. But my hope was that the lengthy discussion of the individualism of self-fulfilment would stake out the lines of a general stance towards modernity which could perhaps be extended to the other zones of malaise as well. In this section, I'd like to try to indicate briefly what this would involve for the threatened dominance of instrumental reason.

In regard to authenticity I have been suggesting that the two simple, extreme positions, of the boosters and the knockers, respectively, are to be avoided; that root-and-branch condemnation of the ethic of self-fulfilment is a profound mistake, as is a simple global endorsement of all its contemporary forms. I have argued that there is a tension between the underlying ethical ideals and the ways these come to be reflected in people's lives, and this means that a systematic cultural pessimism is as misguided as a global cultural optimism. Rather, we face a continuing struggle to realize higher and fuller modes of authenticity against the resistance of the flatter and shallower forms.

Something analogous holds for instrumental reason, my second main area of concern. Here, too, there are extreme positions. There are people who look on the coming of technological civilization as a kind of unmitigated decline. We have lost the contact with the earth and its rhythms that our ancestors had. We have lost contact with ourselves, and our own natural being, and are driven by an imperative of domination that condemns us to ceaseless battle against nature both within and around us. This complaint against the "disenchantment" of the world has been articulated again and again since the Romantic period, with its sharp sense that human beings had been triply divided by modern reason — within themselves, between themselves, and from the natural world.[52] It is present in our culture today in a number of forms. It goes along, for instance, with an admiration for the life of pre-industrial peoples, and often with a political position of defence of aboriginal societies against the encroachment of industrial civilization. It is also a major theme in one strand of the feminist movement, linked with the claim that the dominating stance to nature is "male," and is an essential feature of "patriarchal" society.

People with this outlook square off against the out-and-out boosters of technology, who think there is a fix for all our human problems, and are impatient of those who stand in the way of development out of what appears to be obscurantist unreason.

An analogously polarized debate is easy to find here. But there is an important difference: the alignments are not the same. Crudely put, the knockers of authenticity are frequently on the right, those of technology on the left. More pertinently, some (but not all) of those who are critical of the ethic of self-fulfilment are great supporters of technological development, while many of those who are deeply into the contemporary culture of authenticity share the views about patriarchy and aboriginal styles of life I just adverted to. These cross-alignments even lead to some troubling contradictions. Right-wing American-style conservatives speak as advocates of traditional communities when they attack abortion on demand and pornography; but in their economic policies they advocate an untamed form of capitalist enterprise, which more than anything else has helped to dissolve historical communities, has fostered atomism, which knows no frontiers or loyalties, and is ready to close down a mining town or savage a forest habitat at the drop of a balance sheet. On the other side, we find supporters of an attentive, reverential stance to nature, who would go to the wall to defend the forest habitat, demonstrating in favour of abortion on demand, on the grounds that a woman's body belongs exclusively to her. Some adversaries of savage capitalism carry possessive individualism farther than its most untroubled defenders.

These two polarized debates are very different, but nevertheless I think that both are more or less equally wrong. The sacrifices that runaway instrumental reason imposes on us are obvious enough, in the hardening of an atomistic outlook, in our imperviousness to nature. There the knockers are right. Yet we can't see the development of technological society just in the light of an imperative of domination. Richer moral sources have fed it. But as in the case of authenticity, these moral sources tend to get lost from view, precisely through the hardening of atomist and instrumentalist values. Retrieving them might allow us to recover some balance, one in which technology would occupy another place in our lives than as an insistent, unreflected imperative.

Here again, there could be a struggle between better and worse modes of living technology, as there is between higher and lower ways of seeking authenticity. But the struggle is inhibited, in many cases it fails altogether to begin, because the moral sources are covered over and lost from sight. And in this occlusion the knockers have their part, because their relentless description of technological society in terms of domination screens out these other sources altogether.

But the boosters are no help either, because they tend to have bought so deeply into the atomist and instrumentalist stance that they too fail to acknowledge these sources. As with authenticity, both sides in the polarized debate are in an unwitting conspiracy to keep something essential from view, to accredit the lowest view of the thing they do battle over — in this case, instrumental reason. Against them, we need to do a work of retrieval, in order to get a fruitful struggle going in our culture and society.

Before engaging in this retrieval, there is a point that we can't avoid. To a considerable degree the dominance of instrumental reason is not just a matter of the force of a certain moral outlook. It is also the case that in many respects we find ourselves pushed to give it a large place in our lives, as I mentioned at the beginning of this book. In a society whose economy is largely shaped by market forces, for example, all economic agents have to give an important place to efficiency if they are going to survive. And in a large and complex technological society, as well as in the large-scale units that make it up — firms, public institutions, interest groups — the common affairs have to be managed to some degree according to the principles of bureaucratic rationality if they are to be managed at all. So whether we leave our society to "invisible hand" mechanisms like the market or try to manage it collectively, we are forced to operate to some degree according to the demands of modern rationality, whether or not it suits our own moral outlook. The only alternative seems to be a kind of inner exile, a self-marginalization. Instrumental rationality seems to be able to lay its demands on us coming and going, in the public or the private spheres, in the economy and the state, in the complementary ways that those two great analysts of modernity, Marx and Weber, have explained.

Now this is very true and important. It helps to account for the power of atomistic and instrumental attitudes and philosophies in our time. Atomism in particular tends to be generated by the scientistic outlook that goes along with instrumental efficiency, as well as being implicit in some forms of rational action, such as that of the entrepreneur. And so these attitudes acquire almost the status of norms, and seem backed by unchallengeable social reality.

But people have gone on from this to claim that there is something ineluctable about the atomist-instrumental outlook once one has entered our kind of society. If this were so, then much of what I have been saying in previous sections would be without interest, because I have been and will be exploring reasons to limit the scope of instrumental considerations, and this assumes that we have the power to do so. It supposes that we have a real choice here, even if we tend to be blind to the options open to us. If it really is the case that modern technological society locks us into an "iron cage," then all this is so much wasted breath. This is the third major challenge to my entire argument, which I outlined at the end of section II, but have not yet properly adressed.

I think that there is a great deal of truth in these "iron cage" pictures. Modern society does tend to push us in the direction of atomism and instrumentalism, both by making it hard to restrict their sway in certain circumstances and by generating an outlook that takes them for granted as standards. But I believe that the view of technological society as a kind of iron fate cannot be sustained. It simplifies too much and forgets the essential. First, the connection between technological civilization and these norms is not unidirectional. It's not just that the institutions breed the philosophy; the outlook also had to begin to have some force in European society before the institutions could develop. Atomist and instrumentalist outlooks had begun to spread among at least the educated classes of western Europe and America before the Industrial Revolution. And, indeed, Weber saw the importance of this ideological preparation for modern capitalism.

But that may be dismissed as of purely historical interest. Maybe there had to be philosophical change for our technological society to arise, but once here it constrains us nonetheless. This is one plausible interpretation of what Weber was trying to say with his image of the iron cage.

But this seems to be vastly oversimple as well. Human beings and their societies are much more complex than any simple theory can account for. True, we are pushed in this direction. True, the philosophies of atomism and instrumentalism have a head start in our world. But it is still the case that there are many points of resistance, and that these are constantly being generated. We need think only of the whole movement since the Romantic era, which has been challenging the dominance of these categories, and of the offshoot of that movement today, which is challenging our ecological mismanagement. That this movement has made some headway, has made some dent, however incipient and inadequate, in our practices stands as a partial refutation of any iron law of technological society.

The recent history of this movement tells us a lot about both the limits and the possibilities of our predicament. A fragmented public, divided in its concerns, is indeed at the mercy of what seems like an ineluctable fate pushing towards the dominance of instrumental reason. Each little fragment may deeply care about some bit of its environment threatened with destruction or degradation in the name of development. But it seems that in this each local community or group of concerned citizens stands over against the vast majority of the public, demanding a sacrifice in development, and hence GNP per head, for that public, in the name of their minority interest. So formulated, the case seems hopeless: it is politically a lost cause, and it doesn't even seem to deserve to win. The mills of democratic politics ineluctably grind such small islands of resistance into powder.

But once a climate of common understanding comes to be created around the threat to the environment, the situation changes. There remain, of course, battles between local groups and the general public. Everyone sees the need for a dump, but no one wants it in their back yard. Nevertheless, some local battles come to be seen in a new light, they come to be differently enframed. The preservation of some wilderness areas, for instance, the conservation of some threatened species, the protection against some devastating assaults on the environment come to be seen as part of a new common purpose. As so often is the case, the mechanisms of inevitability work only when people are divided and fragmented. The predicament alters when there comes to be a common consciousness.

We don't want to exaggerate our degrees of freedom. But they are not zero. And that means that coming to understand the moral sources of our civilization can make a difference, in so far as it can contribute to a new common understanding.

We are not, indeed, locked in. But there is a slope, an incline in things that it is all too easy to slide down. The incline comes from the institutional factors mentioned above, but also from a bent in the ideas themselves. We saw something like this in the case of authenticity, as I tried to show in section VI: a way in which the moral ideals lend themselves to a certain distortion, or selective forgetting.

Something of the same is true for the case of instrumental rationality, and for partly overlapping reasons. I have described some of the sources for the strength in our culture of an ideal of self-determining freedom. We are free when we can remake the conditions of our own existence, when we can dominate the things that dominate us. Obviously this ideal helps to lend even greater importance to technological control over our world; it helps to enframe instrumental reason in a project of domination, rather than serving to limit it in the name of other ends. In fact, it has contributed to neutralize some of the limits that still existed to runaway technological devastation of the environment, as the recent history of Marxist-Leninist societies has shown, ideologically powered as they were by a form of this ideal.

Instrumental reason has also grown along with a disengaged model of the human subject, which has a great hold on our imagination. It offers an ideal picture of a human thinking that has disengaged from its messy embedding in our bodily constitution, our dialogical situation, our emotions, and our traditional life forms in order to be pure, self-verifying rationality. This is one of the most prestigious forms of reason in our culture, exemplified by mathematical thinking, or other types of formal calculation. Arguments, considerations, counsels that can claim to be based on this kind of calculation have great persuasive power in our society, even when this kind of reasoning is not really suited to the subject matter, as the immense (and I think undeserved) saliency of this type of thinking in social sciences and policy studies attests. Economists dazzle legislators and bureaucrats with their sophisticated mathematics, even when this is serving to package crude policy thinking with potentially disastrous results.

Descartes was the most famous early spokesman of this mode of disengaged reason, and he took a fateful step that has been widely followed since. We might think of this mode of reasoning as an achievement worth aiming at for certain purposes, something we manage to attain part of the time, even though constitutionally our thought is normally embodied, dialogical, shot through with emotion, and reflects the ways of our culture. Descartes took the step of supposing that we *are* essentially disengaged reason; we are pure mind, distinct from body, and our normal way of seeing ourselves is a regrettable confusion. One can perhaps see why this picture appealed to him and to those who have followed. The ideal seems to gain force and authority when we suppose that it is how we *really are*, as against the objective of attempts at rather fragile and local achievement. So it is all too easy for us in our culture to think of ourselves as essentially disengaged reason. This explains why so many people find it quite unproblematic that we should conceive human thinking on the model of the digital computer. This self-image is enhanced by the sense of power that goes along with a disengaged instrumental grasp of things.

So a lot, both institutionally and ideologically, is going for atomism and instrumentalism. But, if my argument is right, we can also struggle against it. One of the ways we can do so is by retrieving some of the richer moral background from which the modern stress on instrumental reason took its rise. I can't develop the argument here, even to the sketchy extent that I did for authenticity, but I would like to indicate briefly how it might go.

It is obvious that part of what is going for instrumental reason is that it enables us to control our environment. Domination does speak to us, whether just because we can get more of what we want, or because it flatters our sense of power, or because it fits with some project of self-determining freedom. But the "domination of nature" is not the whole story here, as some of the critics seem to imply. There are two other important moral contexts that I would like to mention here, from which the stress on instrumental reason has arisen.

(1) We have already seen that it is linked with a sense of ourselves as potentially disengaged reason. This is grounded in a moral ideal, that of a self-responsible, self-controlling reasoning. There is an

ideal of rationality here, which is at the same time an ideal of freedom, of autonomous, self-generating thought.

(2) Another moral strain has entered the picture. What I called the affirmation of ordinary life, the sense that the life of production and reproduction, of work and the family, is what is important for us, has also made a crucial contribution, for it has made us give unprecedented importance to the production of the conditions of life in ever-greater abundance and the relief of suffering on an ever-wider scale. Already in the early seventeenth century, Francis Bacon criticized the traditional Aristotelian sciences for having contributed nothing "to relieve the condition of mankind."[53] He proposed in their stead a model of science whose criterion of truth would be instrumental efficacy. You have discovered something when you can intervene to change things. Modern science is in essential continuity in this respect with Bacon. But what is important about Bacon is that he reminds us that the thrust behind this new science was not only epistemological but also moral.

We are heirs of Bacon, in that today, for instance, we mount great international campaigns for famine relief or to help the victims of floods. We have come to accept a universal solidarity today, at least in theory, however imperfect our practice, and we accept this under the premiss of an active interventionism in nature. We don't accept that people should continue to be potential victims of hurricanes or famines. We think of these as in principle curable or preventable evils.

This practical and universal benevolence also gives a crucial place to instrumental reason. Those who react against the place it has come to take in our lives on aesthetic or lifestyle grounds (and this has been a large part of the protest over the decades since the eighteenth century) are often taxed by defenders with being morally callous and unimaginative, putting their own aesthetic sensibility above the vital needs of masses of suffering people.

So instrumental reason comes to us with its own rich moral background. It has by no means simply been powered by an overdeveloped *libido dominandi*. And yet it all too often seems to serve the ends of greater control, of technological mastery. Retrieval of the richer moral background can show that it doesn't need to do this, and indeed that in many cases it is betraying this moral background in doing so — analogously to the way the more self-centred modes of self-fulfilment betray the ideal of authenticity.

What this retrieval would involve is essentially the same as in the case of authenticity. We need to bring together two orders of considerations. Drawing on (a) the conditions of human life that must condition the realization of the ideals in question, we can determine (b) what the effective realization of the ideals would amount to.

We can see what this kind of reflection involves if we look at one important example, from the field of medical care. Under (a), we note that the ideal of disengaged reason must be considered precisely as an ideal and not as a picture of human agency as it really is. We are embodied agents, living in dialogical conditions, inhabiting time in a specifically human way, that is, making sense of our lives as a story that connects the past from which we have come to our future projects. That means (b) that if we are properly to treat a human being, we have to respect this embodied, dialogical, temporal nature. Runaway extensions of instrumental reason, such as the medical practice that forgets the patient as a person, that takes no account of how the treatment relates to his or her story and thus of the determinants of hope and despair, that neglects the essential rapport between cure-giver and patient — all these have to be resisted in the name of the moral background in benevolence that justifies these applications of instrumental reason themselves.[54] If we come to understand why technology is important here in the first place, then it will of itself be limited and enframed by an ethic of caring.

What we are looking for here is an alternative enframing of technology. Instead of seeing it purely in the context of an enterprise of ever-increasing control, of an ever-receding frontier of resistant nature, perhaps animated by a sense of power and freedom, we have to come to understand it as well in the moral frame of the ethic of practical benevolence, which is also one of the sources in our culture from which instrumental reason has acquired its salient importance for us. But we have to place this benevolence in turn in the framework of a proper understanding of human agency, not in relation to the disembodied ghost of disengaged reason, inhabiting an objectified machine. We have to relate technology as well to this very ideal of disengaged reason, but now as an ideal, rather than as a distorted picture of the human essence. Technology in the service of an ethic of benevolence towards real flesh and blood people; technological, calculative thinking as a rare and admirable achievement of a being who lives in the medium of a quite different kind of thinking: to live instrumental reason from out of these frameworks would be to live our technology very differently.[55]

Although there is a bent or slide towards the stance of dominance, for all the reasons mentioned above, nothing says that we *have* to live our technology this way. The other modes are open. The prospect we face here is a struggle, in which these different modes of enframing contend. With authenticity, the contest was between flatter and fuller modes of self-fulfilment; here it pits the different frameworks against each other. Once again, I am proposing that instead of seeing our predicament as fated to generate a drive for ever-increasing technological control, which we will then either rejoice at or bemoan depending on our outlook, we understand it as open to contestation, as a locus of probably unending struggle.

In this contest understanding our moral sources can count, and once again the polarized debate between boosters and knockers threatens to deprive us of a crucial resource. That's why a work of retrieval here is worthwhile. There is a battle for hearts and minds in which it has a role to play.

But it is also true that this battle of ideas is inextricably bound up, part source and part result, with political struggles about the modes of social organization. Given the importance of our institutions in generating and sustaining an atomist and instrumental stance, it could not be otherwise. And so I want to turn in my last section to the third main area of concern that I outlined at the beginning.

X
AGAINST FRAGMENTATION

I argued in the preceding section that the institutions of a technological society don't ineluctably impose on us an ever-deepening hegemony of instrumental reason. But it is clear that left to themselves they have a tendency to push us in that direction. That is why the project has often been put forward of leaping out of these institutions altogether. One such dream was put forward by classical Marxism and enacted up to a point by Leninism. The goal was to do away with the market and bring the whole operation of the economy under the conscious control of the "associated producers," in Marx's phrase.[56] Others cherish the hope that we might be able to do without the bureaucratic state.

It is now evident that these hopes are illusory. The collapse of Communist societies has finally made undeniable what many have felt all along: market mechanisms in some form are indispensable to an industrial society, certainly for its economic efficiency and probably also for its freedom. Some people in the West rejoice that this lesson has finally been learned and make the end of the Cold War a pretext for the celebration of their own utopia, a free society ordered through and through by impersonal market relations, with the state pushed into a limited residual role. But this is equally unrealistic. Stability, and hence efficiency, couldn't survive this massive withdrawal of government from the economy, and it is doubtful if freedom either could long survive the competitive jungle that a really wild capitalism would breed, with its uncompensated inequalities and exploitation.

What should have died along with communism is the belief that modern societies can be run on a single principle, whether that of planning under the general will or that of free-market allocations. Our challenge is actually to combine in some non-self-stultifying fashion a number of ways of operating, which are jointly necessary to a free and prosperous society but which also tend to impede each other: market allocations, state planning, collective provision for need, the defence of individual rights, and effective democratic initiative and control. In the short run, maximum market "efficiency" may be restricted by each of the other four modes; in the long run, even perhaps economic performance, but certainly justice and freedom, would suffer from their marginalization.

We can't abolish the market, but nor can we organize ourselves exclusively through markets. To restrict them may be costly; not to restrict them at all would be fatal. Governing a contemporary society is continually recreating a balance between requirements that tend to undercut each other, constantly finding creative new solutions as the old equilibria become stultifying. There can never be in the nature of the case a definitive solution. In this regard our political situation resembles the cultural predicament I described earlier. The continuing cultural struggle between different outlooks, different enframings of the key ideals of modernity, parallels on the institutional level the conflicting demands of the different but complementary ways we organize our common life: market efficiency may be dampened by collective provision through the welfare state; effective state planning may endanger individual rights; the joint operations of state and market may threaten democratic control.

But there is more than a parallel here. There is a connection, as I have indicated. The operation of market and bureaucratic state tends to strengthen the enframings that favour an atomist and instrumentalist stance to the world and others. That these institutions can never be simply abolished, that we have to live with them forever, has a lot to do with the unending, unresolvable nature of our cultural struggle.

Although there is no definitive victory, there is winning or losing ground. What this involves emerges from the example I mentioned in the previous section. There I noted that the battle of isolated communities or groups against ecological desolation was bound to be a losing one until such time as some common understanding and a common sense of purpose forms in society as a whole about the preservation of the environment. In other words, the force that can roll back the galloping hegemony of instrumental reason is (the right kind of) democratic initiative.

But this poses a problem, because the joint operation of market and bureaucratic state has a tendency to weaken democratic initiative. Here we return to the third area of malaise: the fear articulated by Tocqueville that certain conditions of modern society undermine the will to democratic control, the fear that people will come to accept too easily being governed by an "immense tutelary power."

Perhaps Tocqueville's portrait of a soft despotism, much as he means to distinguish it from traditional tyranny, still sounds too despotic in the traditional sense. Modern democratic societies seem far from this, because they are full of protest, free initiatives, and irreverent challenges to authority, and governments do in fact tremble before the anger and contempt of the governed, as these are revealed in the polls that rulers never cease taking.

But if we conceive Tocqueville's fear a little differently, then it does seem real enough. The danger is not actual despotic control but fragmentation — that is, a people increasingly less capable of forming a common purpose and carrying it out. Fragmentation arises when people come to see themselves more and more atomistically, otherwise put, as less and less bound to their fellow citizens in common projects and allegiances. They may indeed feel linked in common projects with some others, but these come more to be partial groupings rather than the whole society: for instance, a local community, an ethnic minority, the adherents of some religion or ideology, the promoters of some special interest.

This fragmentation comes about partly through a weakening of the bonds of sympathy, partly in a self-feeding way, through the failure of democratic initiative itself. Because the more fragmented a democratic electorate is in this sense, the more they transfer their political energies to promoting their partial groupings, in the way I want to describe below, and the less possible it is to mobilize democratic majorities around commonly understood programs and policies. A sense grows that the electorate as a whole is defenceless against the leviathan state; a well-organized and integrated partial grouping may, indeed, be able to make a dent, but the idea that the majority of the people might frame and carry through a common project comes to seem utopian and naive. And so people give up. Already failing sympathy with others is further weakened by the lack of a common experience of action, and a sense of hopelessness makes it seem a waste of time to try. But that, of course, *makes* it hopeless, and a vicious circle is joined.

Now a society that goes this route can still be in one sense highly democratic, that is egalitarian, and full of activity and challenge to authority, as is evident if we look to the great republic to our south. Politics begins to take on a different mould, in the way I indicated above. One common purpose that remains strongly shared, even as the others atrophy, is that society is organized in the defence of rights. The rule of law and the upholding of rights are seen as very much the "American way," that is, as the objects of a strong common allegiance. The extraordinary reaction to the Watergate scandals, which ended up unseating a president, are a testimony to this.

In keeping with this, two facets of political life take on greater and greater saliency. First, more and more turns on judicial battles. The Americans were the first to have an entrenched bill of rights, augmented since by provisions against discrimination, and important changes have been made in American society through court challenges to legislation or private arrangements allegedly in breach of these entrenched provisions. A good example is the famous case of *Brown vs the Board of Education*, which desegregated the schools in 1954. In recent decades, more and more energy in the American political process is turning towards this process of judicial review. Matters that in other societies are determined by legislation, after debate and sometimes compromise between different opinions, are seen as proper subjects for judicial decision in the light of the constitution. Abortion is a case in point. Since *Roe vs Wade* in 1973 greatly liberalized the abortion law in the country, the effort of conservatives, now gradually coming to fruition, has been to stack the court in order to get a reversal. The result has been an astonishing intellectual effort, channelled into politics-as-judicial-review, that has made law schools the dynamic centres of social and political thought on American campuses; and also a series of titanic battles over what used to be the relatively routine — or at least non-partisan — matter of senatorial confirmation of presidential appointments to the Supreme Court.

Alongside judicial review, and woven into it, American energy is channelled into interest or advocacy politics. People throw themselves into single-issue campaigns and work fiercely for their favoured cause. Both sides in the abortion debate are good examples. This facet overlaps the previous one, because part of the battle is judicial, but it also involves lobbying, mobilizing mass opinion, and selective intervention in election campaigns for or against targeted candidates.

All this makes for a lot of activity. A society in which this goes on is hardly a despotism. But the growth of these two facets is connected, part effect and part cause, with the atrophy of a third, which is the formation of democratic majorities around meaningful programs that can then be carried to completion. In this regard, the American political scene is abysmal. The debate between the major candidates becomes ever more disjointed, their statements ever more blatantly self-serving, their communication consisting more and more of the now famous "sound bytes," their promises risibly unbelievable ("read my lips") and cynically unkept, while their attacks on their opponents sink to ever more dishonourable levels, seemingly with impunity. At the same time, in a complementary movement, voter participation in national elections declines, and has recently hit 50 per cent of the eligible population, far below that of other democratic societies.

Something can be said for, and perhaps a lot can be said against, this lop-sided system. One might worry about its long-term stability, worry, that is, whether the citizen alienation caused by its less and less functional representative system can be compensated for by the greater energy of its special-interest politics. The point has also been made that this style of politics makes issues harder to resolve. Judicial decisions are usually winner-take-all; either you win or you lose. In particular, judicial decisions about rights tend to be conceived as all-or-nothing matters. The very concept of a right seems to call for integral satisfaction, if it's a right at all; and if not, then nothing. Abortion once more can serve as an example. Once you see it as the right of the fetus versus the right of the mother, there are few stopping places between the unlimited immunity of the one and the untrammelled freedom of the other. The penchant to settle things judicially, further polarized by rival special-interest campaigns, effectively cuts down the possibilities of compromise.[57] We might also argue that it makes certain issues harder to address, those that require a wide democratic consensus around measures that will also involve some sacrifice and difficulty. Perhaps this is part of the continuing American problem of coming to terms with their declining economic situation through some form of intelligent industrial policy.[58] But it also brings me to my point, which is that certain kinds of common projects become more difficult to enact where this kind of politics is dominant.

An unbalanced system such as this both reflects and entrenches fragmentation. Its spirit is an adversarial one in which citizen efficacy consists in being able to get your rights, whatever the consequences for the whole. Both judicial retrieval and single-issue politics operate from this stance and further strengthen it. Now what emerged above from the example of the recent fate of the ecological movement is that the only way to countervail the drift built into market and bureaucracy is through the formation of a common democratic purpose. But this is exactly what is difficult in a democratic system that is fragmented.

A fragmented society is one whose members find it harder and harder to identify with their political society as a community. This lack of identification may reflect an atomistic outlook, in which people come to see society purely instrumentally. But it also helps to entrench atomism, because the absence of effective common action throws people back on themselves. This is perhaps why one of the most widely held social philosophies in the contemporary United States is the procedural liberalism of neutrality that I mentioned earlier (in section II), and which combines quite smoothly with an atomist outlook.

But now we can also see that fragmentation abets atomism in another way. Because the only effective counter to the drift towards atomism and instrumentalism built into market and bureaucratic state is the formation of an effective common purpose through democratic action, fragmentation in fact disables us from resisting this drift. To lose the capacity to build politically effective majorities is to lose your paddle in mid-river. You are carried ineluctably downstream, which here means further and further into a culture enframed by atomism and instrumentalism.

The politics of resistance is the politics of democratic will-formation. As against those adversaries of technological civilization who have felt drawn to an elitist stance, we must see that a serious attempt to engage in the cultural struggle of our time requires the promotion of a politics of democratic empowerment. The political attempt to re-enframe technology crucially involves resisting and reversing fragmentation.

But how do you fight fragmentation? It's not easy, and there are no universal prescriptions. It depends very much on the particular situation. But fragmentation grows to the extent that people no longer identify with their political community, that their sense of corporate belonging is transferred elsewhere or atrophies altogether. And it is fed, too, by the experience of political powerlessness. And these two developments mutually reinforce each other. A fading political identity makes it harder to mobilize effectively, and a sense of helplessness breeds alienation. There is a potential vicious circle here, but we can see how it could also be a virtuous circle. Successful common action can bring a sense of empowerment and also strengthen identification with the political community.

This sounds like saying that the way to succeed here is to succeed, which is true if perhaps unhelpful. But we can say a little more. One of the important sources of the sense of powerlessness is that we are governed by large-scale, centralized, bureaucratic states. What can help mitigate this sense is decentralization of power, as Tocqueville saw. And so in general devolution, or a division of power, as in a federal system, particularly one based on the principle of subsidiarity, can be good for democratic empowerment. And this is the more so if the units to which power is devolved already figure as communities in the lives of their members.

In this respect, Canada has been fortunate. We have had a federal system, which has been prevented from evolving towards greater centralization on the model of the United States by our very diversity, while the provincial units generally correspond with regional societies with which their members identify. What we seem to have failed to do is create a common understanding that can hold these regional societies together, and so we face the prospect of another kind of loss of power, not that we experience when big government seems utterly unresponsive, but rather the fate of smaller societies living in the shadow of major powers.

This has ultimately been a failure to understand and accept the real nature of Canadian diversity. Canadians have been very good at accepting their own images of difference, but these have tragically failed to correspond to what is really there. It is perhaps not an accident that this failure comes just when an important feature of the American model begins to take hold in this country, in the form of judicial review around a charter of rights. In fact, it can be argued that the insistence on uniform application of a charter that had become one of the symbols of Canadian citizenship was an important cause of the demise of the Meech Lake agreement, and hence of the impending break-up of the country.[59]

But the general point I want to draw from this is the interweaving of the different strands of concern about modernity. The effective re-enframing of technology requires common political action to reverse the drift that market and bureaucratic state engender towards greater atomism and instrumentalism. And this common action requires that we overcome fragmentation and powerlessness — that is, that we address the worry that Tocqueville first defined, the slide in democracy towards tutelàry power. At the same time, atomist and instrumentalist stances are prime generating factors of the more debased and shallow modes of authenticity, and so a vigorous democratic life, engaged in a project of re-enframing, would also have a positive impact here.

What our situation seems to call for is a complex, many-levelled struggle, intellectual, spiritual, and political, in which the debates in the public arena interlink with those in a host of institutional settings, like hospitals and schools, where the issues of enframing technology are being lived through in concrete form; and where these disputes in turn both feed and are fed by the various attempts to define in theoretical terms the place of technology and the demands of authenticity, and beyond that, the shape of human life and its relation to the cosmos.

But to engage effectively in this many-faceted debate, one has to see what is great in the culture of modernity, as well as what is shallow or dangerous.

As Pascal said about human beings, modernity is characterized by *grandeur* as well as by *misère*. Only a view that embraces both can give us the undistorted insight into our era that we need to rise to its greatest challenge.

Notes

1. Alexis de Tocqueville, *De la Démocratie en Amérique* vol. 2 (Paris: Garnier-Flammarion, 1981), p. 385.

2. "Erbärmliches Behagen"; *Also Sprach Zarathustra*, Zarathustra's Preface, sect. 3.

3. Tocqueville, *De la Démocratie*, p. 127.

4. For the absurdities of these calculations, see R. Bellah et al., *The Good Society* (New York: Knopf, 1991), pp. 114–19.

5. Bellah et al., *The Good Society*, chapter 4.

6. See especially Patricia Benner and Judith Wrubel, *The Primacy of Caring: Stress and Coping in Health and Illness* (Menlo Park, CA. Addison-Wesley, 1989).

7. Albert Borgman, *Technology and the Character of Contemporary Life* (Chicago: University of Chicago Press, 1984), pp. 41–42. Borgman even seems to echo Nietzsche's picture of the "last men" when he argues that the original liberating promise of technology can degenerate into "the procurement of frivolous comfort" (p. 39).

8. Hannah Arendt, *The Human Condition* (Garden City, NJ: Doubleday, Anchor Edition, 1959), p.83.

9. Tocqueville, *De la Démocratie*, p. 385.

10. See for instance R. Bellah et al., *Habits of the Heart* (Berkeley: University of California Press, 1985).

11. This image occurs in Bloom, *The Closing of the American Mind* (New York: Simon and Schuster, 1987): "The loss of the books has made them narrower and flatter. Narrower because they lack what is most necessary, a real basis for discontent with the present and awareness that there are alternatives to it. They are both more contented with what is and despairing of ever escaping from it. . . . Flatter, because without interpretations of things, without the poetry or the imagination's activity, their souls are like mirrors, not of nature, but of what is around" (p. 61).

12. Bloom, *The Closing of the American Mind*, p. 84.

13. See John Rawls, *A Theory of Justice* (Cambridge: Harvard University Press, 1971), and "The idea of an overlapping consensus," in *Philosophy and Public Affairs* 17 (1988); Ronald Dworkin, *Taking Rights Seriously* (London: Duckworth, 1977) and *A Matter of Principle* (Cambridge: Harvard University Press, 1985); also Will Kymlicka, *Liberalism, Community and Culture* (Oxford: The Clarendon Press, 1989).

14. I have written about this at greater length in *Sources of the Self* (Cambridge: Harvard University Press, 1989), chapter 3.

15. See especially Alasdair MacIntyre, *After Virtue* (Notre Dame: University of Notre Dame Press, 1981) and *Whose Justice? Which Rationality?* (Notre Dame: University of Notre Dame Press, 1988).

16. Of course, for a certain vulgar Marxism, the negative answer is quite explicit. Ideas are the product of economic changes. But much non-Marxist social science operates implicitly on similar premises. And this in spite of the orientation of some of the great founders of social science, like Weber, who recognized the crucial role of moral and religious ideas in history.

17. Individualism has in fact been used in two quite different senses. In one it is a moral ideal, one facet of which I have been discussing. In another, it is an amoral phenomenon, something like what we mean by egoism. The rise of individualism in this sense is usually a phenomenon of breakdown, where the loss of a traditional horizon leaves mere anomie in its wake, and everybody fends for themselves — e.g., in some demoralized, crime-ridden slums formed by newly urbanized peasants in the Third World (or in nineteenth-century Manchester). It is, of course, catastrophic to confuse these two kinds

of individualism, which have utterly different causes and consequences. Which is why Tocqueville carefully distinguishes "individualism" from "egoism."

18. See David Harvey, *The Condition of Post-modernity* (Oxford: Blackwell, 1989).

19. Bloom, *The Closing of the American Mind*, p. 25.

20. The development of this doctrine, at first in the work of Francis Hutcheson, drawing on the writings of the Earl of Shaftesbury, and its adversarial relation to Locke's theory, I have discussed at greater length in *Sources of the Self*, chapter 15.

21. "Le sentiment de l'existence dépouillé de toute autre affection est par lui-même un sentiment précieux de contentement et de paix qui suffiroit seul pour rendre cette existence chère et douce à qui sauroit écarter de soi toutes les impressions sensuelles et terrestres qui viennent sans cesse nous en distraire et en troubler ici bas la douceur. Mais la pluspart des hommes agités de passions continuelles connoissent peu cet état et ne l'ayant gouté qu'imparfaitement durant peu d'instans n'en conservent qu'une idée obscure et confuse qui ne leur en fait pas sentir le charme." Rousseau, *Les Rêveries du Promeneur Solitaire*, Ve Promenade, in *Oeuvre Complètes*, vol. 1 (Paris: Gallimard, 1959), p. 1047.

22. "Jeder Mensch haat ein eigenes Mass, gleichsam eine eigne Stimmung aller seiner sinnlichen Gefühle zu einander." Herder, *Ideen*, vii.I., in *Herders Sämtliche Werke*, vol. XIII, ed. Bernard Suphan, 15 vols. (Berlin: Weidmann, 1877–1913), p. 291.

23. I have developed this view of moral reasoning at greater length in "Explanation and Practical Reason," Wider Working Paper WP72, World Institute for Development Economics Research, Helsinki, 1989.

24. George Herbert Mead, *Mind, Self and Society*, (Chicago: Chicago University Press, 1934).

25. This inner dialogicality has been explored by M.M. Bakhtin and those who have drawn on his work. See of Bakhtin, especially, *Problems of Dostoyevsky's Poetics* (Minneapolis: University of Minnesota Press, 1984); and also Michael Holquist and Katerina Clark, *Michail Bakhtin* (Cambridge: Harvard University Press, 1984), and James Wertsch, *Voices of the Mind* (Cambridge: Harvard University Press, 1991).

26. See Bakhtin, "The Problem of the Text in Linguistics, Philology and the Human Sciences," in *Speech Genres and Other Late Essays*, ed. Caryl Emerson and Michael Holquist (Austin: University of Texas Press, 1986), p. 126, for this notion of a "super-addressee," beyond our existing interlocutors.

27. "If a person possesses any tolerable amount of common sense and experience, his own mode of laying out his existence is the best, not because it is the best in itself, but because it is his own mode." John Stuart Mill, *Three Essays* (Oxford University Press, 1975), p. 83.

28. This point is forcefully made in R. Bellah et al., *Habits of the Heart*.

29. Gail Sheehy, *Passages: Predictable Crises of Adult Life* (New York: Bantam Books, 1976), pp. 364, 513. (Italics in original.)

30. R. Bellah et al. Note the connection between this kind of individualism and procedural justice in *Habits*, pp. 25–26.

31. I have discussed this whole turn of modern culture at greater length in *Sources of the Self*, especially in chapter 13.

32. Montesquieu, "La nature de l'honneur est de demander des préférences et des distinctions"; *De l'Esprit des Lois*, Livre III, chapter vii.

33. The significance of this move from "honour" to "dignity" is interestingly discussed by Peter Berger in his "On the Obsolescence of the Concept of Honour," in Stanley Hauerwas and Alasdair MacIntyre, eds., *Revisions: Changing Perspectives in Moral Philosophy* (Notre Dame:

University of Notre Dame Press, 1983), pp. 172–81.

34. Rousseau is describing the first assemblies. "Chacun commença à regarder les autres et à vouloir être regardé soi-même, et l'estime publique eut un prix. Celui qui chantait ou dansait le mieux; le plus beau, le plus fort, le plus adroit ou le plus éloquent devint le plus considéré, et ce fut là le premier pas vers l'inégalité, et vers le vice en même temps." *Discours sur l'Origine et les Fondements de l'Inégalité parmi les Hommes* (Paris: Granier-Flammarion, 1971), p. 210.

35. See for example the passage in the "Considerations sur le Gouvernement de Pologne" where he describes the ancient public festival, in which all the people took part, in *Du Contrat Social* (Paris: Garnier, 1962), p. 345; and also the parallel passage in "Lettre à D'Alembert sur les Spectacles," ibid., pp. 224–25. The crucial principle was that there should be no division between performers and spectators, but that all should be seen by all. "Mais quels seront enfin les objets de ces spectacles? Qu'y montrera-t-on? Rien, si l'on veut. . . . donnez les spectateurs en spectacles; rendez-les acteurs eux-mêmes; faites que chacun se voie et s'aime dans les autres, que tous en soient mieux unis."

36. See *The Phenomenology of Spirit*, chapter 4.

37. The connection between Derrida's anti-humanism and a radical, untrammelled sense of freedom emerges in passages like the one alluded to here, where he describes his mode of thinking as one that "affirms free play and tries to pass beyond man and humanism, the name man being the name of that being, who throughout the history of metaphysics or of ontotheology — in other words, through the history of all of his history — has dreamed of full presence, the reassuring foundation, the origin and end of the game." Derrida, "Structure, Sign, and Play in the Discourse of the Human Sciences," in Richard Macksey and Eugenio Donato, eds., *The Structuralist Controversy* (Baltimore: Johns Hopkins University Press, 1972), pp. 264–65.

38. Michel Foucault, interview, in H. Dreyfus and P. Rabinow, *Michel Foucault: Beyond Structuralism and Hermeneutics* (Chicago: University of Chicago Press, 1983), pp. 245, 251.

39. I have discussed expressivism at greater length in *Hegel* (Cambridge: Cambridge University Press, 1975), chapter 1, and in *Sources of the Self*, chapter 21.

40. Friedrich Schiller, *On the Aesthetic Education of Man*, trans. Elizabeth Wilkinson and L.A. Willoughby, bilingual edition (Oxford: The Clarendon Press, 1967).

41. I have discussed the relation between these two ideas at length in *Hegel* (Cambridge: Cambridge University Press, 1975).

42. See the interesting article by Vincent Descombes on *Foucault: A Critical Reader*, ed. David Hoy (Oxford: Blackwell, 1986), in *The London Review of Books*, March 5, 1987, p. 3, where he discusses the rather different perceptions of Foucault in the United States and in France; and also Jürgen Habermas, *The Philosophical Discourse of Modernity*, trans. Frederick G. Lawrence (Cambridge, Mass.: MIT Press, 1987).

43. I have tried to develop a much fuller account of this as well as other strands of the modern identity in *Sources of the Self*.

44. The tremendous popularity of two books, in both cases a little to the surprise of their authors, attests to this. One is Bloom's *The Closing of the American Mind*, which I have been discussing. The other is Paul Kennedy's *The Rise and Fall of the Great Powers* (New York: Random House, 1987), which is precisely about the loss of quasi-imperial status. I should also mention a Canadian film, *Le déclin de l'empire Américain*, which also played into this cultural pessimism, and which, uncharacteristically for a Québécois film, was quite a hit south of the border.

45. Earl Wasserman, *The Subtler Language* (Baltimore: Johns Hopkins University Press, 1968), pp. 10–11.

46. Thus Wordsworth tells us of how he

> would stand
> If the night blackened with a coming storm,
> Beneath some rock, listening to notes that are
> The ghostly language of the ancient earth
> Or make their dim abode in distant winds.
>
> (*The Prelude*, *ℓ*.307–11)

47. Charles Rosen and Henri Zerner, *Romanticism and Realism* (New York: Norton, 1984), p. 58. This chapter (2) contains an excellent discussion of the Romantic aspiration to a natural symbolism.

48. Rosen and Zerner, *Romanticism and Realism*, pp. 68ff.

49. Quoted in Rosen and Zerner, *Romanticism and Realism*, p. 67. Rosen and Zerner relate this to a statement by Constable: "For me, painting is only another word for feeling."

50. Borgman, *Technology and the Character of Contemporary Life*, chapter 11.

51. See Rousseau, *Les Rêveries du Promeneur solitaire*, Ve Promenade, in *Ouevres Complètes* (Paris: Gallimard, 1959), p. 1045.

52. I have developed the account of these divisions at greater length in *Hegel*.

53. Francis Bacon, *Novum Organum*, I.73, translation

from *Francis Bacon: A Selection of His Works*, ed. Sydney Warhaft (Toronto: Macmillan, 1965), pp. 350–51.

54. I have drawn a lot on the penetrating discussion in Benner and Wrubel, *The Primacy of Caring*, which shows how much philosphy can contribute to a new enframing of instrumental reason of the kind I am discussing here.

55. The issue I am putting here in terms of alternative modes of enframing is sometimes posed in terms of control: does our technology run away with us, or do we control it, put it to our purposes? But the problem with this formulation should be obvious. It remains entirely within the frame of domination, and doesn't allow for a quite different placing of technology in our lives. Getting on top of technology implies taking an instrumental stance to it, as we through it do to everything else. It doesn't open the possibility of placing technology within a non-instrumental stance, as we see, for instance, in an ethic of care, or a cultivation of our capacity for pure thought. On this issue, see the discussion in William Hutchinson, "Technology, Community and the Self," Ph.D. thesis, McGill University, 1992.

In this discussion of enframing, I have obviously borrowed a great deal from Heidegger; see especially "The Question Concerning Technology," in *The Question Concerning Technology and Other Essays*, trans. William Lovitt (New York: Garland Publishers, 1977). What I take Heidegger to be proposing in this and other writings is something like what I have called an alternative enframing. For an interesting development of this idea in much greater detail, which also owes a debt to Heidegger, see Borgman, *Technology and the Character of Contemporary Life.*

56. "Freedom in this field can only consist in socialized man, the associated producers, rationally regulating their interchange with Nature, bringing it under their common control, instead of being ruled by it as by the blind forces of Nature." *Capital*, vol. III (New York: International Publishers, 1967), p. 820.

57. Mary Ann Glendon, *Abortion and Divorce in Western Law* (Cambridge: Harvard University Press, 1987) has shown how this has made a difference to American decisions on this issue, as compared with those in comparable Western societies.

58. I have raised the issue about democratic stability in "Cross-Purposes: The Liberal-Communitarian Debate," in Nancy Rosenblum, ed., *Liberalism and the Moral Life* (Cambridge: Harvard University Press, 1989). There is a good discussion of the slide towards this lop-sided package in American politics in Michael Sandel, "The Procedural Republic and the Unencumbered Self," in *Political Theory* 12 (February 1984). I have compared the American and Canadian systems in this respect in "Alternative Futures," in

Alan Cairns and Cynthia Williams, eds., *Constitutionalism, Citizenship and Society in Canada* (Toronto: University of Toronto Press, 1985). There is a good critique of this American political culture in B. Bellah et al., *Habits of the Heart* (Berkeley: University of California Press, 1985) and *The Good Society* (New York: Knopf, 1991).

59. I have discussed this at greater length in "Shared and Divergent Values," in Ronald Watts and Douglas Brown, eds., *Options for a New Canada* (Kingston: Queen's University Press, 1991).

Index